Introduction

On the 15th of October 2011, the 'Occupy' movement of Amsterdam burst fruitfully into manifestation. The big demonstration on the Place de la Bourse was the big bang, jets of nutritious citrus spray bursting out in all kind of strange and inconceivable directions. A week later, unless I am mistaken, the Beursplien square held 100 tents. I was in Brighton, United Kingdom, Planet Earth. It seems people, globally, had been tuning into these strange feelings of INJUSTICE for some time, to the point where people you perhaps never thought could ever be interested or compassionate towards such and such a human concern, were breathing heat so potent, that you were scared for your hair. It was fantastic. Was this the first real positive universal achievement of the internet? To spread the news and raise the consciousness to the point where enough of the population were aware enough to not only recognise that we have long been conned by the global financial system and large corporation (which as is now fairly commonly known, benefits only the minority), but to stand up together and say "No", "we won't take this any more", "our rights are our rights".

Occupy 'Wall Street' in Zuccotti Park, New York had started a month earlier (September 17th), and was receiving much media coverage. I believe 'Occupy' wall street had a huge influence on the worldwide events of October 15th, but the main catalyst for the Occupy movement, in any of its guises, can be traced back to the revolutionary fuelled series of protests and demonstrations in the Arab world, which began on the 18th December 2010 and were named 'Arab Spring'. In England, my hub, Occupy London emerged on the 15th October, the same day demonstrations were taking place in **900** cities throughout the world. A fact that just purely amazes me. From Tokyo to Sao Paulo, Sydney to Berlin, people were taking to the streets to vent their frustrations. For me, in regards to the United Kingdom, the pendulum seemed to have been swinging in the direction of something like 'Occupy' for a fair while. There had been a series of protests in the year or two leading up to it (one memorably marred by the mindless dropping of a fire extinguisher from a central london building, which the media obviously got their fangs deep in to, diverting the positivity), and despite locational difficulties after a failed attempt to occupy the London stock exchange, it began quietly and heavily blowing around its word.

Shock and disbelief were zipping into peoples eyes and ears not only from down the road, but from down the phone line, through the internet cable. We were seeing. We still continue to this day to share in the grief, suffering, and the occasional breakthrough and joy of our fellow humans, our brothers and sisters from all parts of the world and from all walks of life, as we sculpture and action more and more refined tools to shatter the shackles around our ankles. I feel like we are just beginning to reconnect and share with each other once more, realising that our similarities are abundant and our differences are to be celebrated. Anyway, however the blanket of humanity was being restitched, it was, just as it is, and by the 9th of October 2011 Occupy protests had taken place and/or were ongoing in a reported 95 cities, in 82 countries, and over 600 communities in the United States. Something was building, was rising.

So many people seemed to be feeling those bullets of INJUSTICE. You know, that kind of injustice that teeters around your brain in minuscule tunnels, with pristine effort, like a cunning, greedy little mice, the kind of injustice that makes sure it leaves you plenty of YOUR OWN brain function to get on with your day, and after conversing with you, actually makes you believe that it is doing you a favour by leaving you that much, of your own function that is. Yes this is a type of injustice, perhaps its the main kind of injustice in the typical western world? Don't get me wrong, people of the western world are still hungry, millions probably, and there is no excuse for that just as there is no excuse for any of it, but my point is that the main outcry and desire of people, such as people in a province such as Amsterdam in the early second decade of the 21st century, is not one for water, for food, for basic necessity, (although, as this book will explain, I am very aware that these basic necessities can always turn into matters of need, whether you live in the western world, the eastern world or any world). It is more a cry, in my opinion, for our minds to be dusted and our bottoms to be wormed, in order for us to be rid of all the conscious and unconscious poison and venom that has swept through and continues to sweeps through society. Through the society of the city, the town, the village, even the hamlet, leaving its wretched manifest marks, such as soulless advertisement, exploitation, love blocking illusion, poorly woven shoes and profit minded pies, crafted in the absence of love. Some of these unsustainable threads are obviously not weak, they take, and will continue to take a great deal of de-knotting if we are to eliminate them from group mind and consciousness. However, we hold the key of personal action, and I believe it is self and group action that holds (as it has throughout history) the true power, the power that leads to the positive universal change and each baby step forward for our race.

On one of the first mornings of November 2011, I sailed from England to Holland in search of some relief from the repetitions of my steady and fun, yet increasingly spiritually unfulfilling life in Brighton. On the 6th of November, due in part to the Beurspliene campsite being too small to facilitate the needs of the movement, a group of Occupy protestors peacefully squatted an old derelict (for 15 years may I add) laboratory across the canal to Buiksloterweg, behind Amsterdam train station. The aptly nicknamed 'Great laboratory' had once been one of, if not THE main constructs of power for the Shell oil company. I believed, and still believe, that the initial aim of squatting the building was to develop a network of community projects that could be facilitated within and around the grounds of the building, as well as the building providing peaceful and sustainable living for a community of like minded individuals. I spent a week in Amsterdam with my ex girlfriend before she returned to England and I was due to travel on through Europe for a month or two. That was not to be. Due to various interesting influences I was to spend that time in Amsterdam, as a child who felt like he was finally standing up for himself, his rights, and his beliefs. "Viva la Revolution!" I believe my first contact with the Shell building was a brisk evening around the 12th November. I moved in the next day.

What follows here-on-in is an insight into and a journey through, MY time spent with occupy, in the shell, with those beautiful sandy souls that made some pearls and treated them as animate objects, which they were. Those bright shiny altruistic pearls that summoned us, dazzled us, and held us inside of its ecosystem for a decent duration, despite the scraping of the sandy bed on our knees, and the filtration of the leaked trawler oil into our family home through its aged wrinkles and cracks.

I invite you to walk with me, if you will, around the beauty of Amsterdam, around the meanderings and musings of mild mind, of maddened mind, of all mind I encountered (including mine), around miscommunication, around ego, around sub greed, around chakra imbalances and around the night time shadows of the 'Groot Laboratorium'.

Little too often do we find ourselves inside of a state of consciousness where we can see through enough of our own greedy, self rewarding and individualistic ego, to remember that we are WITH them that we are sometimes told and feel that we are APART from, and that within each and every one of our own individualistic and communal microcosms, our POWER is still INFINITE, and its all too deliciously and divinely grand. Infinitely radiant. I feel that my time with Occupy gave me the chance to see through my own 'crap' so to speak, giving my eyes a slightly deeper and richer field of vision, not dissimilar to the kind of positive effects reportedly induced by psychotropic plants, just without them...

For everyone…

✱✱✱✱✱✱✱

Struggling for tea-lights,
They're not hoarding on those surely?
"Why don't you get out of here you cave-krettin"
"No way mmaaaann, dam you! Be I chief kraker"

"What is your name and favourite colour?" This had been the first, and pleasant, question of the general assembly meeting. "And why is it your favourite colour?" This was shortly prior to the ensuing arguments. The question was to be passed, clockwise if my memory serves me true, around the circle of flicking fire and silhouette faces, as the baby flames worked their little shifts for the occupy cause. The question never reached me anyway, I don't even think I got the chance to sweat it a little, but what shit would I have spouted anyway?

It may have been:

'Purple, oh I must say purple, for this correlates strong with my crown, just atop of my pineal, through which the spirits of the clever ones feed me, oh how glorious, what an honour, it is my pleasure and privilege to be your dodgy radio you delightful sentient beings. I do hope you trust me with some more, and some greater ideas soon'

No, save the heavier stuff for later, for a 3am humanity fuelled heart to heart exchange with my next occupied door neighbour, if they allowed me to stay of course. To be honest I would probably have just blurted out a quick nervous answer.

'Pen and Burple'

But I never got to splutter, emotional ego and anger stopped the spin, they encompassed. Shoulders back, chest out, 'I can lead', 'this can be MY fantasy!' These thoughts were being thought, maybe everyone had individual playful visions? The hero, the heroic idea, mythology, Joseph Campbell, the leggy princess, chastity belts, the sparkling pearl! But some peoples visions seemed to be going too far! what on earth was occurring right here? We have a problem, a void, a lack of something:

Com-pro-mise
n.
1.
a. A settlement of differences in which each side makes concessions.

b. The result of such a settlement.
2. Something that combines qualities or elements of different things

Occupy?
Community project?
Cultural centre?

MY occupy to the right, OUR occupy to the left. A good two and a half thirds of us want to skip through the woodland shortcut in the middle, because we know its the only direction that furthers humanity. So we put on our comfiest, most durable boots, and start helping each other with the lacing. Alas the last half a third unlace again, when we aren't looking, when we are making our sandwiches and filling our flasks for the pilgrimage. They slip our slippers back on, thinking they are helping, knowing they aren't, or merely not thinking.

So many intricacies, bloody deluded individualistic egos, I know only mine, in vague, but I see ramifications of the rest that I feel are not just merely projections of myself. Unexalted ego I mean:

In you rush with your unexalted ego,
and smash the window your fellow prole will have to fix once more
tomorrow,
same lowly wage,
as the man you wished to attack is informed of your thuggery as a passing
comment on the lower end of a briefing paper,
handed to him by his wanking hand secretary,
as he sips his frappuccino in a revolting slurp,
and thinks of the youthful saliva of the cash hungry teenage girls mouth
orifice only.
No,
we need more guile,
more consciousness,   <<<<<<<< <<<<<<<<<<   <<<<<<<<<   *thus*
togetherness,
5 and three quarter billion minds are stronger than the remainder,
lets win the rest over,
and no,
I desire not to lead us in,
when we tune in and listen instead of tuning out and ignoring in the state
we falsely label: BLISS,
we will just know,
our spirits will guide,
our nature will tell,
revelations abundant,
confusing a little at first,
then beautiful,

beautiful and peaceful,
incomprehensibly so.

As I was saying, they shouted, stood, puffed up, floated, spat rotten air, filled the room with a dank odour that lurked and crawled consciously and un, up everyones nostrils and into the mind waves. The frequency slowed, we were less able to touch and play the notes of love.
  The caveman squeezed out of the door, lingered in the stoned, breathy hall:

"He's taken copper!" one accused.

"No it was gone!" one defended.

"No he is gone!" another thrusted.

"No you should go!" a shadow joined.

Anyway, I never got to stutter Pen or Burple.

★★★★★★

It was Alex that led me to the shell building, i'd seen the tent camp on a late night/early morn jaunt to the Beursplein square, i'd heard they were there. I had intended to go to London, but some malfunction lead to the campsite being erected directly outside St Paul's cathedral, 'like a big swanky phallic finger straight up the nose of western tradition. The beautiful and misunderstood western tradition, downtrodden and segmented,

"here you go altruistic church tradition, take that"
"up yours spirit and divinity!" ("Your own spirit and divinity" splutters the higher self from a higher diving board).

  It seemed like a bad place for it anyway, but I would make a guess that most of the people involved on the day the camp was seeded were only too aware of it. The original plans to camp outside the London Stock Exchange had been unsuccessful and the camp outside St Paul's was an alternative, a hurried alternative as it had to be. In trying to see the positive, maybe this led to other camp formations around London. I know that to this day the Occupy London group are still holding meetings, events and actions, with all that knowledge that has passed around since that giant penis was flashed at St Paul, so to speak. This is not to say that there were not logistical difficulties in Amsterdam also, on the 28th October a second site was opened in Amsterdam (though it was to be quickly shut down by the police), due to lack of space and problems with apparent 'alcohol related nuisance' at the Beursplien. Yet it still appeared to me that the Beursplien campsite didn't inhibit its neighbours quite so much as the St Paul's assembly. Ah, the good old Dutch. There was an excitement, a buzz. Banners everywhere:

'OCCUPY – brought to you by: HYPO, REAL ESTATE GROUP, BAYERN LB, DEXIA, BRADFORD AND BINGLEY, COMMERZBANK'

The sarcastic satirical tongue in full wag, the channelled anger against a restricted playground and unloving ideals that seem to install themselves like growing leeches. Why does it feel as though such a hefty handful of our species, for one reason or another, gradually decide that becoming a creature of ignorance is the easiest way for us to live? It amazes me how such little regard is to often paid to the complexities that blossom over time, when we choose to ignore the little unsightly manifestations we see, hear and feel. Do we forget them to try and engage in a somewhat tainted, instant, malnourished "peace of mind"?

Our generation, the one prior and then beforehand and then again prior, at some point, have had the little, dirty, soiled puddles splash to their faces, and chosen to simply wash it off and forget, when maybe sometimes the puddle should have been cleaned, to stop the next passer by from getting a face full of the same scum. But we didn't have time, we were late for the meet, Tommy needed catching from the playground, Derek wanted you to check over the report, mmm reports, with your finest toothcomb, before tomorrow minst...

...and who heard of cleaning a puddle, what would that do? Let some tell you some theories:

It could be done as an act of love, and the purity of the thought would enter into the collective consciousness, raising its frequency. The more acts of love we all demonstrate, the higher the concentration. The higher the concentration, the higher the frequency, the higher the frequency of love in the collective consciousness, the less people will fear, and the less people fear, the more likely they are to manifest symbols and acts of love. Acts of love that will benefit humanity, and thus themselves. We may not always see how, maybe the explanations are just beyond our current conscious understanding, but we are getting at the same goal, all of us, i'm so sure of it. In our deepest depths we crave happiness, we look out from our perches, with different angles and perspectives, and have different ideas of what happiness is. Yet we are all connected to the soul of this world, we lay on the body of this world, and we all (sometimes unfortunately) affected by the microcosms and macrocosms of group mind, as we tread the fruitful and the thorny paths of this world. We all tie together inside a beautiful super silk ribbon.

When the puddle is a lagoon and has been growing scum for some time, it starts to really hum. It is putrid, and it is then that we think we might try seeing to it. We all ignore and avoid sometimes, if we don't we realise just how inconceivably mad it all is, and then most of them call you mad. So you tend not to keep looking at how mad it all really is, or it grabs you, and maddens you further, straddling a whole fresh branch of madness, at a tremendous height (Blocked toilets are we not?) I feel it is this failure to hold concentration that allows the sneaky bastards to package their vomits without eyes to witness actions.

This anger I speak through is not one that cares that someone has more money or resources than its regulator. I don't believe my anger to be over protective of me at all really. I am happy for someone who works hard and ethically (and by ethically do I solely mean humanely?) for their extensive amounts of paper tokens. I encourage it in fact. Go on, treat yourself, be aware of the materialism that waits in the wings, trying to invoke detrimental ramifications for you, but eat a greater majority of the box, please, I insist, just make sure you leave enough for everyone else though eh, I like the white ones and the strawberry creams. Mindfulness. Don't take a mans meal and make it into a piece of high brow, pointless, contemporary art. Choose HUMAN. Don't take a mans shelter and trade it over into another convertible, like an unsightly soulless contemporary transformer. Choose HUMAN. Does this not go without saying? Is my delusion that onset? Please stop it, stashing handfuls and handfuls of food in your pockets simply for you and yours only. Shit, look at the size of the queue. Look I said please, now just stop it. Cut it down, down and down to fade out. Mindfulness.

Sorry, as I was rambling, it's not pure equality I am wishing to drive at, "he has a fair few quids more than me, what the....hoohah-blarta-evenkeeldemocracy-tothepenny-tothemax", no its not someone else having more than me that scrapes my heart, its as follows:

Why do I keep seeing so many energetic, artistic, intelligent, playful, bubbly, human and loving ideas, borne of sights to the desire of an alternative way of life and 'work'.....halted? Halted (delayed) from encouraged and wilful manifestation, by bureaucratic delusion, by narrow mindedness, by miserliness, by buy buy.

I propose my version of why, it will make me feel better, I'll get it off my chest, again.

- There are too many pockets of power manifesting personal gains.
- This kind of power can't listen, and if it can't listen then it will never understand, it is a yellow bellied, narrow minded busy body, eating as its belly pops and sprays oil (55%), gristle (20%), dirt (20%) and herpes (5%) to the back of our throats so soon as we intimate to gulp.
- This type of power has built what it deems to be a handy and clever by-pass, right around the frequencies of love and of harmony.

This twisted strain of power that keeps offloading its shit into me is a power with an awful ego problem, desperate delusion and many suggestions of deep rooted psychological complexes. When you think of it, it is more weakness than power, it is only power in Maya (illusion), and we can't count fully on a part truth, but we do, that's why were in this riddle. Oh the poor old human mind, sheltered from so much knowledge and conscious understanding, like the cotton wrapped newborn kicking around to crawl, to stand, to no avail. I would now go as far as to propose that the term power has taken on predominantly 'control centred' connotations, such is the state of the world we live in and the lack of compassion in our general global structure. How can this be right?

POWER - "The ability to do something or act in a particular way, esp. as a faculty or quality". Oh, how good would it be to take the predominant usage back towards this meaning. Ah, imagine what it would mean if our foremost collective connotation of the word was more in line with this definition.

Whilst I am on the subject of lost terms, may I mention the likes of SQUATTER and HIPPIE.

HIPPIE - "seekers of meaning and value"."connoting awareness"

SQUATTERS - Often very politically minded people looking for an alternative way of life. In Amsterdam, for example, since the criminalisation of squatting, many squatters are missed by locals immensely. They created opportunities i.e. artist workplaces, stages for performance art, organisation of alternative events. They implemented empathy, charity, compassion, and chiefly: Humanity. Robyn Hud was a criminal to those who looked at him as thus. Take from that what you will, but try not to take it from the poor, or the nearly poor for that matter. What they possess extra in cash, they appear all too oft prone to spending away, in their ill guided quest to keep up with Robinson's.

Pure, clean ghosts of the terms wander streets so hard, yet not impossible, to navigate. May we set our compasses? We toyed with our compasses' as cubs, remind me where we start again.
★★★★★★★
This thing I shall loosely label 'CONTEMPORARY POWER' : It reacts in a snarl with term 'greed', in a 60 minute makeover laboratory that used to be a child's bedroom, producing the synthesised hybrid 'GROWER' (greed/power), that keeps telling the sneaky bastards to keep packaging their vomits.

let me make my point clear, I am not saying that my state should feed me and home me while I'm sat idly on my ass 24/7. Far from it. I have no fear of getting my hands dirty, I just refuse to dip them in shit is all, and shit is what I am given access to (9 and a half times out of 10). Yes, immoral, pure money driven, soulless, monotonous shit, and it becomes more and more concentrated. Seriously, have you ever looked in the job section of the paper, or what about one of those job search machines in a job centre? Well, if you haven't, its the kind of experience where half way through you are checking over your shoulder to see if Jeremy Beadle hasn't risen from his grave to perform one last elaborate wind up "You've been Beadled my boy". Besides, even if I do find something I'm half arsed about, I know that most the rest of my friends and my fellow human brothers are not gonna be so lucky. The final insult is that there isn't even enough of this shit (soulless jobs) to go around, haha, well frig me sidelong. Why would anyone truly believe for one moment that I might be content with this arrangement? Mass unhappiness has a direct bearing upon my happiness. I am pulled into action by sick factions of group mind/s, and it takes a hell of an effort to get the splinters out, I haven't seen tweezers since I got lost in the labyrinths of Boots that day they teamed up with that other big retailer and made a port hole through time and space from one store to another. Why should I accept this shit? How the fuck do we accept this shit? Hell, it affects you, do you accept this shit? Wait, who are you? And who/what is it that I am even talking about? HHHEEEELLLLLLLLLLLLLOOOOO? Greed? The confused collective consciousness? Is that you? Whoever you are, fuck your minimum wage, the one that stays the same while the shit is pumped out of the price of everything. Inflating as it shrinks. Fuck your dole money, I will leave it, my mind feels purer now without it. Balls to the drone that looked down on me and telling me what I must do, high on her 'Job centre' throne. Your requests of me suck at my creativity and my happiness, my human rights may I propose, and I decline. Yes thats right, fuck my 3 steps towards finding a 'sheep pen' in which to inhabit for 40 hours a week. I have no CONCRETE answers for any of the humane manifestations that I/we could perform, that may be deemed as 'work', in order that we may all, at last, get our fair chances to peacefully manifest our ever developing dreams and ideas, in settings absent of stifling, dogmatic requirement, yet I know that if we weren't talking to an automated telephone representative, perhaps we could, together, fathom some.

Will not the keys for the restoration of our faith, and our lost happiness, need to be contextually cut as situations arise. Subjective to our celebrated individuality, they will desire loving decisions at each time of **now**. We will clearly not find our answers in this corrupt capitalist system as it stands, or in: socialism, communism, republicanism, or the ever entangling, ramified branch of getting fucked-up-ism. Spin an eye back on paganism, reflect on pantheism, contemplate animism, and we might find some rough tools with which to work, and, in my humble opinion, I believe we start to get a little warmer. Thus said, It is pretty clear, to my eyes, that our answers are not to be found, confined, inside of any ism, or any formulated and man made doctrinal outlay. One thing I feel certain of is that love and happiness cannot even begin to withstand any kind of political system with soggy, soiled and sordid ulterior agendas, such as those that largely govern us today. Governments, and perhaps moreover, the invisible (though increasingly visible) puppeteers behind governments, contain heavy corruption and inhumanity throughout the world, we know this now, it's out, its transparent (thank you at last Mr and Mrs internet, perhaps I misconceived you somewhat). It can't be hidden from us any more, and that which is still hidden, will someday be unearthed, such is the power of truth. Haha. The financial system as we currently know it has crumbled, we know this too. Virtual beef is all. The answers and ways out are not in any kind of individual doctrinal idea. Perhaps the answers are something like constantly changing sliding plates, interlocking and separating in unconscious grace, like Luigi of the Mario Brothers, stepping forward just as the platforms join for a second, as he bumbles unawares of his footwork, eyes closed, in a daydream about princesses groin, his happy thought. Seriously though, we can't read how to be and how to act. Is it not that we need to get in touch, or keep in touch with our hearts? altruistic feelings? Instincts? Look and search inwardly? Will we not find our answers gradually? Slowly unfolding, pulled by the forces of a love for humanity, our relatively untouched/forgotten divine nature, an ability for local and general compromise, and the strength and willingness to elect respect and LOVE, in its many guises, as our leader.

I simply want help and support along my OWN path, and for YOU to be helped along yours! is it really so much to ask? The paths that fit with our own personal ethics and motivations. I merely demand not to be forced into work and actions that dispute the qualities that I possess or have chance of coming to possess (ill allowing my own nurture), just so I can feed and live and be part of a pre-mystoric, contradictory system. The contradictory system that has manifested from the culmination of all the scum of every puddle, every lagoon, that omits foul odour. Every stale mass that we did not bother to clean out for the past however many years. Am I not being subjected to a glorified slavery if my path to my own nature is blocked, damn fucking right I am. Whether you can understand what the hell i'm trying to babble about or not, whether you think its 'airy fairy juvenile dreamer bollocks or whether you know way more about what I might be babbling on about than I ever will, I just want to live by my floating beliefs, with a peace of mind that I feel I have not been allowed to encounter yet, due, at least in part to, unacceptable environmental and external restriction.

Wait a minute, I'm winding myself up here, why the fuck are we not being readily helped already? I have probably already answered this to the best of my ability but ooohhhhh I tell you, I still don't comprehend, think we've got a dodgy line mate, you'll call back when, yes when hell freezes over, thought so. Seriously though, why are we not helping each other more, are we all just so pumped full of fear that we are that disconnected, scared to be humane? what the fuck is wrong with us, where's our compassion, where went the love? certainly not gone, merely buried a little deep. But we can find it, for sure, we just need to turn around and see the beauty again. What's distracting us anyway, really? Eastenders is shit and Emmerdale unbearable.

★★★★★★

"But how do we get started on these paths you 'HIPPIE' freeloader?. you SCROUNGING squatter?

"We are already on it by the mere positive thought toward it"

"You want free money or something for your journey? What should you be paid for?

"I only use your money because you won't allow me to get on without it, and I will only use it so long as I have to. This word pay is too tightly bound to money. Free it. What should I be paid for? Hhhmmmm, lets see, pay me for what you think of my expression, oh you don't like my expression? Fair enough, well pay me for my positivity then, pay me in mini chocolate buttons. Pay me for care outside of myself, pay him three times as much on that count, pay me in granny smith apples, or jazz ones, pay me for the good energy I give away or something, we must have some means to measure that with our technology, if we don't lets design it, TOGETHER (bless Bill Hicks), Pay me in a meaningful smile, pay me because I lent a friend a book and he changed his street into a giant bouncy castle, pay me because I eased the mind of a beautiful natured old lady with poor feet, whose peace of mind was inhibited by a shabby pigeons feet that had become embroiled in a cotton reel. For all her longing she couldn't help the poor creature, so she offered me the scissors, and I accepted, I tried my darndest to cut the restriction, why? because I could try, because I was there, because I didn't want to turn the cheek, because I gave an ounce of a god dam shit, pay me for that, I deserve it, pay me, don't keep me waiting anymore. Pay me in knowledge, pay me in knowhow, pay me in cloth. I don't know, use your imagination. Pay me by telling me a story of a cloud you drew in your head on a day off from your greed hassled fury. Pay me in inspiration, in hope, and lets build a statue in memory of Eric Arthur Blair out of our newly expired coin collections, on a dusty little side road, somewhere just outside the province of Bihar, then raise our glasses and shed an emotive tear a piece for a fine humanitarian. Pay us by just putting down what you know in your heart wrong, oh I don't fucking well know, pay us by coming to terms naturally with, and without such a carbon footprint, your hideous complexes. I have a major hunch the universe awaits with an ever increasing eagerness to help us from there on in.

These soil and oil and excess vomit scattered puddles are really smelly now, the rain has tried in vein to wash anew, its gotten intolerable, a big clean up is upon us, whether we want it or not. We catch a whiff every time we take the route to the haul, even when our headphones transfer us.

Yet there is hope, we are finally realising that we may need to get down on our hands and knees and work out an ingenious, instinctive (who knows maybe even untried) methods of cleaning the liquids stale. And this is where movements such as 'Occupy" start to plant their virgin feet into those fuzzy, murky depths.

****

We got to the shuttle boats behind Amsterdam central about 7ish probably (PM) , it was pitch black anyway, and cold, I'd been busking:

"Rock me mamma like a wagon wheel,
rock me mamma any way you feel,
heeeeeeyyyyyyy, mamma rock me"

The busking had gone well. Better than I'd anticipated to be honest, it had seemed to carry a certain synchronicity. I'll explain. My lady had left for England in the morning, as planned. Farewells, man I hate farewells. I arrived back at the hostel, as I'd booked one more night. I sat up on my bed in the attic, no good, I descended the stairs and sat at the table near the window, enjoying the view as the sun looked happy administering his vitamin D. The streets were clean, well put together. This was a good neighbourhood. I was out east in Zeeburg, somewhere a few blocks over It was playtime and I could hear the children's laughter and exciting. I am always warmed by such audio, it reminds me that there is still such purity and innocence in the world. That's it, so long as people keep popping out sprogs there will always be purity in this world, always a certain pureness of heart.

I felt at ease for 5 minutes, but no, I had to go back to town, something/someone was urging me there. I'd just wasted two euros on the bus ride back but it mattered little. I'd go and try my hand at a little busking, surely that would help shift my attentions. I popped my guitar in its case and left the hostel. Stepping out into the biting air, which had felt so much warmer inside of glass, I reached full appreciation that I was at a loose end. Should I head east? I had a friend in Germany, Mr Black, who it would be amazing to see. That was the plan anyway, wasn't it? To travel around for a bit. I remembered the lines I scribbled as I sat on the floor of the train with all my bags a week earlier:

Creeping out of Brighton, it begins,
as it has begun so many times before.
I said goodbye to fondant faces in the nature,
with old football flicks of the left boot, rusty.
I feel a tainting of a place I hold dear,
a tainting of people and areas acting up, from suppression.
To refresh is to clean without to much conscious thought.

Yes I wanted to move around for a little while to give myself the fresh perspective I knew I needed once more. Were my perceptions towards Brighton intrinsic? Extrinsic? Ah yes ,of course, BOTH, but which were leaning more heavily towards which? And which was which again? I hoped that moving around would help me clear up some loose ends. So, ok, maybe I should go and book a train towards Berlin, maybe I could get even further east and see Poland at last. Krakow is supposed to be sublime, and of course Warsaw. I felt a rush of excitement. Sitting down on the bus I tried to halt my thinking, as I always do, to no avail. I was starting to become vaguely familiar with the route back to Centrum. After a few minutes of looking out of the window I looked around. A seemingly delightful lady sat near the front of the bus, across from me, her young son at her side. Just as I looked over the little boy looked at me, I smiled at him, he frowned back at me, then looked away. I felt, not offended, but unnerved by the exchange. Somehow my mood flipped, like something was incomplete. Like there was work to be done. I didn't want the little boy to frown, I wanted him to smile.

I stepped off the bus outside central station and started wandering south. I was certainly at a loose end, the lady had gone, I was alone at sea, but certainly not for the first time, and besides, I had buoys. I knew all was fine really. I'd raised some sprouts, and mammo and daddo had slipped me a few tomatoes from the greenhouse. There was a key in my pocket for a warm room anytime I saw fit. Things were bearable, thats all that mattered for now. My biggest weight was a few straggling thoughts that dragged on the concrete behind me as I walked, occasionally slipping into the canal and becoming dampened, or getting momentarily caught under a passing cyclists wheels, exasperating their importance for a few moments...but seriously, it was fine. Sure It was cold, damn cold, but dry, and sometimes that can be the warmest in my head.

A yorkshireman's advice to his son:

"See all, hear all, say nowt...."

A yorkshire son's advice to this day:

'See all, hear all, sing loud....'

I will stop saying it in a minute, I guess when I have finally convinced myself, but again, seriously, it was fine, really. I knew it was just another chapter, for me to paint on as best I could, with the brushes I had available. I would work around the anomalies, maybe my left handedness has helped me with that. Even now, as I write this out in draft, I am having to keep the pen from half twisting and leaving me with no nib, but its part of the fun, a bit, isn't it? It blends into a seamless subconscious mind motor programme after a while doesn't it, you can barely notice, like when you finally get used to your new mobile telephone and your texting with one and a half eyes, the other half eye on a badgers rear end, and half of your concentration on David Attenborough's voice. Yes why not, anomalies, throw a few more cogs into the system, make you a better functioning being. They can.

I stopped off at a little canal bridge, southwest-ish, my bearing cogs spinning. I rested my straggling thoughts a little over the bridge rail, and they hung down to dry off a tad. They scampered limply in the delicate breeze. I removed my guitar in the usual fashion, and placed the hat down:

"When you're sitting there,
in your silk upholstered chair,
talking to the rich folks that you know...."

Smiles, but no coins, thats alright though, I thought. I felt no dejection, maybe I would have in Brighton, but this hood was fresh, too much to still see unfurl for dejection. It was a poor place to busk really, I knew that. I was shaking off the cobwebs so to speak, pouring away the nervousness. Could I call it nervousness, maybe not so much these days, but I feel it still every time I perform. Maybe its because its one of the only things I've ever really truly wanted to do. When my kid eyes closed, I was always sat on a stage in the space between my ears. Was there a crowd? I think not maybe. I guess one of my problems is I can never really convince myself entirely that my pants aren't going to fall down once the audience arrives, and a whole army of crabs aren't going to come crawling out of my pubic hair, really bad ones I never knew I had, and the love of my life is in the crowd, and Its clear she's repulsed. Haha. I shouldn't laugh, its a real hindrance sometimes, more so in the past I suppose. I can turn it to my advantage sometimes these days. I used to call it reasonable doubt. Its not that reasonable:

Reasonable doubt
A delusion that rises from the thrill of the stage/circumstance,
a negative side effect,
an earthing wire to the excitement and unpredictable reality of live
performance/circumstance,
another little anomaly to try and work towards laughing at/with,
another cog to the being.

I was ready for somewhere a tad busier. I wandered north on a back road I'd never taken. Fresh, fresh visual stimulation. I arrived eventually on Haarlemmerstraat, a small chunk west of Nieuwendijk, I recognised it immediately. The bar to my left with its rosy faced clientele was called 'Harlem'. I would up my cogs:

"It ain't no use in turning on your light, babe
That light I never knowed,
And it ain't no use in turning on your light, babe
I'm on the dark side of the road...."

Coin to hat...

Coins to hat...

Decent chat...

Coins to hat…

My fingers had cold ache, I was shivering mildly. I'd done well. I was on my last song for sure when he threw 2 coins down, carried on, double checked me:

"Hey man, fancy seeing you here"

It was Alex. I couldn't believe it. We had met three days ago in a coffee shop. It was kind of strange even then because it was the kind of coffee shop I would never have usually entered in a million years: No smoking, deathly clean, huge smiles on the staff that didn't quite sit right, overpriced coffee. You know the place, your'e paying for the sterility, a cousin of Starbucks, just without the guilt of paying into that particular corporate cow. He had made a kind gesture as we sat down. We bought coffee and slurped. As the lady used the ladies, I caught his eye:

"Hows it going?"
"Not bad"
"You?"
"Can't complain"

We tripped through a few more inquisitions before our spades hit something solid:

"I have been part of 'Occupy' for the last couple of weeks, and well, it has become pretty established down at the Beursplein, and so we decided we needed an overspill place. The other day we successfully occupied an old shell laboratory behind Amsterdam central station", He declared with pleasure.

I felt a huge strong wave of excitement pass through me. I sat with my legs folded in the half lotus position (in the palm of his hand), for a few minutes as he injected my hungry veins with little doses of hope. He showed us an internet clip of the move in day. I was sold.

"I can take you there sometime id you like?"

"Seriously? Sounds great"

I was the most excited I had been in a long time. I suggested the idea of moving on to another coffee shop, one where we could have a little smoke. Alex obliged and we moved on down the road. Me and Sammy had been in Amsterdam for a few days at that point, and I was already getting a nice feel for it, again. It caressed me so. 'Home is where a part is', and I'd left little chunks of myself here on previous visits. These little parts seemed to be being magnetically pulled back towards me. I was quite unconscious of it, but they floated slowly, excitedly, to come and join me for a coffee, like friends you haven't seen for years. They rolled delicately over liberated streets, along canals, up and out of coffee shops, carried by long wisps of dancing smoke, through markets and down red lit streets. They slipped through the cracks in the door of the coffee shop we were sat in, criss crossed around table legs, rose slowly up and settled gently in my mug. We carried on speaking and acquainting ourselves, and as we did, I drank down my particularly tasty coffee:

"We better go and see what Lars Von Trier has to say for himself" I uttered.
"Pleasure to meet you brother, love to you" I extended.

Email exchange, check. Hug exchange, check. And we were out and on our way to the cinema. Melancholia was a it read.

****

A couple of days had passed since meeting Alex. I had emailed him the day before but hadn't checked yet for a reply. I stood, guitar in hand. It was my last song for sure if I was to keep my hands from snapping off.

'Clink - link'

It was ever so strange, there he was, out of the blue, adding to the number of coins that my hat occupied:

"Lets grab a drink, my treat" He offered.

I didn't refuse. Into the Harlem bar we went, and it wasn't long before my face turned rosy too. I told Alex how I'd sent him an email the day before. He hadn't read it yet.

"Do you think you might be able to take me over to the shell building like you mentioned the other day?" I asked.

"Sure of course, we can go after these drinks if you like" he answered. Much to my delight.

The shuttle ferries behind central station are like sweet granddads who will run you anywhere, at the drop of a hat. All you have to do is wait up to about five minutes, but there are even screens that tell to the second how long you're going to be stood for, and it's pretty reliable too. Quite the sensation. Our ferry was to Buiksloterweg. As the ferry chugged across the canal Alex insisted that we stood on the outer part of the vessel, in order to take a smoke, something that I was very happy about, not so much for the smoke, but for the feel of the air, the sounds, the visuals, the overall experience. A thick layer of fog covered the surface of the liquid beneath us, only adding significantly to my sense of excitement and anticipation. The Shell building was located about 4 minutes away from where we disembarked the ferry. As we approached, It cut a dark, large, giant shoebox like figure across the evening skyline. The front yard was large, barren and unkempt. It featured various materials including a couple of piles of concrete sheets, and a huge pile of bricks. Potential I thought. There was a bike rack, and Various bikes were scattered neatly around the front door. The entrance was a sliding glass door which was currently closed. Alex knocked on the glass. I felt a tad anxious but my excitement squashed it straight back down. Like a heavyweight boxer annihilating an overly cocky welterweight. A silhouetted figure approached on the other side of the slim glass pane, steaming it mildly with its breath:

"Mike-check" Proclaimed Alex.

This was the password as I was later informed. The dark figure slid the door open a little and checked us up and down:

"Hey, its Alex"

"Hey, ok, come in"

Alex squeezed through the modest crack in the door, and I scampered through quickly after. We walked up a few steps and into a high and open foyer area. It was almost impossible to see anything, just a few torch lights ran scattily around, lighting up various areas intermittently. Alex began speaking to the people that resided in the hallway. I kept myself quiet and hovered back a little, seeing that there were two sofas with a few people sat on around.

"This is my friend Ben"

The man, I had finally seen that it was a man, that let us in said hi, and I uttered the same back. A concerned Australian girl piped up from the sofa:

"Alex, we haven't seen you for a few days, we are having problems with people gaining access to the building, damage is being done, things are being stolen. It's really no good. We don't know everyone in here anymore and not everyone has been accepted into the community through general assembly. We can't just bring people down here. We need to make sure we have good energetic people here, not like some of the people that have been arriving of late. No offence to you Ben, I mean nothing personal, but it's getting out of control"

"Calm down" Alex reacted. "He is a good guy, he wants to get involved, he has ideas to offer"

"Maybe so, but he's still going to have to go through general assembly and meet everyone first" She returned.

"Thats fine" I interrupted, walking over in her direction. "I believe I'm here for the right reasons. I have been following the events of 'Occupy' in London with a hugely sympathising interest for the past couple of weeks. I want to help. When is there a general assembly?"

"In half an hour" she answered, seeming a little more at ease. "You are welcome to come along and introduce yourself if you like"

"Ok thanks, I will" I said.

The tension seemed to settle somewhat. We began chatting to people and a few of us congregated near the front door for a smoke. After a little while Alex turned to me "Come on up and see my room, and we will come back down for general assembly"

He set off up a huge set of pitch black stairs, I followed. We reached the second floor.

"its through here" he spat.

I couldn't see a thing, We had no torch. It gave me such a surreal feeling. We were clearly in a huge stone building, it was cold and echoey. We went through a huge door and continued on before taking a right down a smaller corridor with windows on the left. I couldn't see what was outside, some kind of courtyard I presumed. At the end of the corridor we turned right and entered a room almost immediately opposite:

"This is it" chirped Alex.

"great"

I could sense immediately that the room was large. Alex pulled out a lighter and began firing up various candles that were placed on the sills all around the room. After a minute or two I could just about see what was going on. The room was huge. It was clearly a big old office, carpeted, with plastic cable holders on each wall. The roof was panelled, the kind where you could push each one up if you can jump high enough to reach them. Like the kind you sometimes found in mobile school classrooms. A couple were missing. A huge whiteboard on the left hand wall was scribbled all over with various 'Occupy' tactics', both serious and playful. In the centre of the room was a square table with 3 or 4 chairs strewn randomly around it. The room was on the corner of the building and huge tall windows ran the full length of the two outside walls. Out of one window I could make out a separate part of the building, and from the other I could see city lights in the distance, and what looked like an area that could be grass, but it was difficult to make true sense in this light, or distinct absence of. All I could easily make out was my breath that clouded in front of me. Alex lit a final candle and set it down in the middle of the table:

"Sit down. What do you think? " He questioned.

"Very nice" I grinned.

"It has potential doesn't it?

"Absolutely, its a really decent space"

We sat down and had a smoke.

"How do you feel about general assembly then, you nervous?" he asked.

"A little I guess, I'm quite excited and eager to meet everyone too though"

…..20 or so minutes passed in chat.

"We best head down then" Alex chirped.

"Lets do it!"

We wandered back down on the route that had taken us up, this time with a couple of tea lights each to help. We got back down to the foyer area and this time took a left. We entered, what I think was, the third room on the left. I could see the outline of about 25-30 people sat in a vague circle around the room. It was too dark. Someone commented on the fact as soon as I thought it:

"Yeah, it seems like we're struggling for tea lights" Someone answered.

After a peaceful few minutes the fracas ensued. General assembly was over, almost as soon as it had begun. When the argument finished I looked around the room. Most people looked shocked and threatened by what they had seen. This was something that we shared already. I thought back to my ponderances from earlier in the day when I was leaving the hostel, the ones in which I'd contemplated booking a train over to Germany, and maybe on to Poland. Krakow perhaps. I knew what I should do straight away. I thought about the poetry that had been pouring out of me for the past few years, the late night scribings that vented my anger against things like inequality and totalitarian rule. How amazing would it feel to do something, to be part of something that stood up to such things. I was sat in a dark room, surrounded, barring Alex, by complete and utter strangers, and I now knew why I had felt like there was work to be done when I had seen the frown of the little boy on the bus earlier. At long last maybe I was inside something that had foundations of purpose, finally something to apply my energy to that wasn't about me per se. Something bigger, something stronger. Inside me no doubt, containing me sure, but beyond me, way beyond just me and my own ego. I was exactly where I needed to be. I knew in the blink of an eye that I wanted to be there and endeavour to make as much of a difference as possible.

I carried on looking around the room. Some people had left as soon as the arguments calmed a little and it sank in for sure that the meeting had failed, but about half of the people stayed. Pockets of people had begun chattering amongst themselves. I hadn't muttered a word, just observed. I decided that if I wanted to stay (and oh I wanted to stay), then silence was probably not my strongest tactic. I introduced myself to some people to my left and got into conversation. I continued in this vein for a while.

acquainting myself, and trying to get a deeper feel of what was happening at the same time. It soon dawned on me how diverse the age and the nationality of the people in the room were. It was something that pleased me, although it seemed obvious straight away that there were some spoken language barriers. I just hoped I could stay. After half an hour or so Alex turned to me:

"We are gonna head up and sit in my room for a little while, care to join?"

"Yes of course, one minute" I answered.

I had chatted to her again already, but I decided to re-approach the Australian girl once more.

"I obviously didn't really get chance to introduce myself to everyone during general assembly, but I want to be part of what you are doing here" I announced.

I wouldn't have been surprised if she maybe thought I was a little mad after what I had just witnessed unfold, but she returned politely:

"Well you have met a fair few people here now, which is possibly more than some of the people here to be honest, and no-one seemed to have any problems. Come back tomorrow if you want, its not really up to me, I don't know if I will be here too much longer, but I'm sure its fine."

I ventured back up to Alex's room with him and another dutch guy. I could sense that the other lad was hurt by what he had seen, and he seemed like he was harbouring some anger towards certain people he deemed to be messing things up. It was clear that there were problems. Someone was violent apparently and a threat to people, and the chap who had got them into the building, Dirk, well he was being accused of stealing copper water pipes from the building and selling them on. A giant stained glass window had been broken to a degree. There was work to be done alright. I had no real perspective on things and decided to keep most of my thoughts to myself. We sat, talked and smoked for a little while. After a little while Alex made a suggestion:

"I'm not sure how much I'm gonna be around, you can stay in here if you like."

"Thank you very much brother, thats very good of you" I accepted.

"Well the thing is" He continued. "I have travelled lots of places, and people have always been so kind and helpful to me, so its a pleasure to be able to help out others"

"I like that a lot, and one day I hope to pass that goodness on, and it will be my pleasure too"

****

The next morning arrived as I imagined it may, as my eyes reemerged I stared once more on the insanely tall curtains concealing me in my cocoon, another bright day seeped in from behind, I knew it was deceptive. My feelings were mixed, I still felt alone, but less so. I felt anxious, but the anxiety was surrounded by a spongy layer of excitement. I'd packed up my bits and pieces before bed so headed straight down to the canteen. The tactical loose trousers gave just enough space for some free takeaway to carry over to my new housemates.

I'd overpacked for sure, two suitcases, one doused in books, slowed me somewhat. I sat by the canal next to the bus stop with a chunk of belongings either side of me. As I lit my cigarette, it was probably 10 am. What a place to be at such a time, sun out, the people, the creatures, the walkways, the canals, all of which regaining its breath, fresh from the morning commute. People watching is fun at such a time, not too chaotic, yet not too sparse. "Maybe I should connect with this hour, in such a way, more often" I thought.

I'm not sure who it was who finally let me into the building, there were 4 or 5 people congregated chatting, none looked familiar bar one. Gorka recognised me from the set back sofa:

"Heeyyy Ben, you made it"

"Hey, yeah, how are you? I brought a few supplies from the hostel if anyone is hungry."

I put the fruit and bread on the food table. It really didn't last long. There was no surprise there, they looked hungry, weary, like they needed something, something more than food, but food would have to do for now. The building appeared, to my perception, so different from the night before. Chiefly because my sight wasn't being aided by 3 middle of the range Albert Heijn tea-lights, but it also seemed as though the intimidating, spooky, corporate stonehold was in a less tense, lighter mood. The sun washed through the glass windowing and showed off the disused state of things. This was the kind of place that one of those souped up property experts would prance around for the cameras proclaiming "Potential, oh yes, potential". Potential it had, these were the goggles I needed to see through. I decided to head up to Alex's room, well, my room too. The vastness of the house dawned on me once more. The big wide stone steps, that snaked up, seemed very impressive. Alex had had me spray my name on our door under his before we left the building the night before, and sure enough 'OCCUPY BEN' was there to be read as I dragged my suitcases ever nearer to their destination. Upon entering the room I dropped them where they fell and headed straight for the back wall of windows, delighted to learn that my wish for a back lawn had come true, and what a back lawn, fields and fields of grassland presumably leading the way to Buiksloterweg, and beyond.

I decided to take myself on a tour. The corridor leading off the room was still relatively dark, incase you hadn't already realised, there was no electricity. The building was set in square columns, corridors working you through the middle of off shooting rooms to the outer walls, with views of the courtyard on the inner side of the structure. The same pattern could be found on four floors, and replicated itself identically at least once, to some more rooms, and laboratories on the other side of the building. Alex had already informed me that much of the building had been locked off due to some vandalism and other problems. We were essentially living inside of just one portion of the building, but there was still plenty to acquaint with. I was later to discover that leading off one doorway on the 3rd floor, rose a staircase that led you up into the upper organs of the building, a passageway leading to 3 or 4 more accessible rooms, a dwarf height labyrinth of metal pipes and machinery, and finally, via one of the rooms, the predominantly flat but multi tiered rooftop.

After becoming somewhat acquainted with my surroundings I eventually pottered back on down to the foyer in semi search of people. I spoke once more with Gorka who introduced me to a fellow Englishman by the name of Lucas, a dutch girl called Masha, a chap called Rodrigo (if I recall), and nervous looking chap called Louis. Whilst keeping my cards a few inches from my chest I joined and listened to the conversation. It was clear that the tension of last night had blown over for now, but another dark cloud was likely again soon. Other complaints involved lack of food, direct criticism of certain people, their 'actions', and their 'lack of understanding' / 'effort'. I sensed a little hypocrisy in some things said, but these people were frustrated, and acting in ways that frustrated people do, to vent is to free up some space, but doesn't it sometimes just give things more energy. I catch myself at it often, but I am starting to see how it mostly just adds fuel to my fire, so to speak. It amazes me how we humans like to moan sometimes: "This is shit and that should be done like that and we need to do this and I wanna do that", but when it comes to turning these words to actions, it is more often than not, easier said than done? This is where Gorka was to inspire me so. Now Gorka was an Italian chap of around 30. He sporadically bore the essence of a child in his manner, when he was allowed, or else wore a detached tolerance, when forced to. All in all a very pleasant and warm chap. See, the best thing about a guy like Gorka, is he didn't really care for such words, he didn't let other peoples rambling affect him, but just got on with his business. He would fix things up, help people out and generally go with the moment. The guy built himself a bed out of scrap wood, the boy was a doo-er. Not a reckless doo-er, but a conscientious doo-er, the best kind of doo-er. The kind of person that perhaps we should all refer to the next time we are sat on our arses, feeling sorry for ourselves, yapping the odds, and the time after that too.

As darkness approached a few more bodies seemed to appear from different parts of the building and a big steel drum was filled with wood and set ablaze as the congregation moved more across towards the courtyard. I spoke with a few fresh faces under firelight until I could smoke or bear to utter my name no more. I retreated to the quiet of my new room. It was cold. I pulled on fair few layers of clothing and made myself up a bed in the far right corner, up against the wall. I didn't quite know what I was in for. Maybe an hour passed after I eventually drifted off, before I awoke once more. It was really cold now, now, now it was too cold. I fixed myself a few more layers of clothing and continued a broken sleep until a chunk past sunrise.

✱✱✱✱✱✱✱

Orders for the day: Air bed, duvet, (two duvets?) pillow. Food supplies, more candle supplies. As I descended to the ground floor foyer I heard some commotion. A huge dutch man was pacing the stone floor, only a spanish chap who spoke no Dutch or English was in the vicinity:

"Whats going on" I asked him

"Fucking dog shit, here, look, here, and here, they treat this place with no respect, its not on" he raged.

"Too right" I agreed.

At first I was impressed with his passion to keep the place tidy, but as he kept on I noticed something that that I had less respect for.

"You know what", he went on, "I found this place, a few months ago, I was the first one in here, yep, that was me, the first, I am not having it."

Whilst I still held a respect for his want of respect for the building, there was a certain egotism to his tone and his statements, it was almost as though he believed himself the owner. 'How dare some shitty dog foul up his patch!' As his rant continued it became clear that he was the kind of person to whom you could convey the greatest idea you've ever borne, and he would come right back with a statement about how he once took out a whole gang of troublemakers with his left bicep. He didn't hear your words, you may as well not be there, bar him having no-one else to shoot his shit at if you weren't. What a shame for such a strong passion to be so entangled with such a strand of egotism that it creates wider cracks in the fissures it intended to force closed. I thought once more about the fissures I create in my own life through my own egotism, hypocrisies and projections. When its all me me me, we will lose we we we and we won't see see see.

As Jonathon appeared from the front entrance it gave 'The founder' a more familiar face to shoot his shit at. Having tried for long enough to unsuccessfully have a conversation (as opposed to being preached at), I took the opportunity to move clear and light up a cigarette, on my own, on the arm of the sofa. 'The founder' was still (and still) blasting his unconstructive complaints when an older looking lean man with a long grey ponytail walked in with a huge set of keys, he looked pretty stressed and seemed to be mumbling to himself under his breath. He approached the East corridor doors and began to finger around with his keys some more. It had already become clear to me that this was the entrance point to the laboratories and the other side of the building, that we weren't allowed to access. He began trying out keys with some frustration. I was intrigued as to what lay behind. Eventually he found the key that matched the particular padlock. Click. He pulled the door open. My intrigue grew:

"Are you ok there? I spoke out, "Need a hand at all?"

"Actually, you could go and grab my toolbox from over there" He spluttered, engaging once more afresh upon the key chain in a new quest to open up the the adjacent door to the pair just opened.

"This ones the store room"

clink - tingle - click

"hhhnnnmmmffff"

"So this is the entrance to the labs?" I inquired

"Yup, we had to lock this area off coz someone has smashed up that lab there to the right" he complained

"It ok for me to take a little look-see?"

"Be my guest."

I didn't hesitate. Haha. Mammoth. High school science times a ton, the hub. This is the place where the vile potions were concocted, in eyes of insatiable greed? The engine room, the heartbeat, the playing field, the shitting main stage baby. This is where the seeds grew, plant, grew, bush come fence, wall, separation, greed, control. I was standing in a defunct nucleus, in a rotten root, of one of the most overgrown plants, inside the whole damned world of monopoly capitalism, peeping in on its action. No warrant, no uniform, nor badge, behind the pathetic rotten yellow tape that catches the winter wind and flaps embarrassingly at it to stop it, without any kind of true enough conviction to sustainably succeed. Makes you laugh in the worst kind of way, does it not, to keep spying and feeling the things that someone, or something (e.g. a plan) empowered by someones, has deemed you unfit to see, or more precisely, the someones wish you not to understand. Yes, you can SEE it, just so long as you don't UNDERSTAND, because if you don't understand then you don't see, you see, and even when its right on your plate, in your tap, or when its flashing brightly at you in its sleek font. But wouldn't we feel it? oh shit we FEEL it, you may feel it all over your achey body, oooo the shoulders for sure, prime spot, but that may be tactically accredited to something else, so as to deviate your understanding furthermore. The problem with the practices of deflection and screening however, all you somethings, you news channels, you excuses, you curtained crusaders, is that people DO SEE, and whilst they don't understand at first glance, they see again, then again, then they tell what they see, and its spreads wide and long like the tables of a free buffet, the buffet of the masses, and they chow down on their fried tofu sandwich and think 'Wow, how did I overlook that last time, and then they guzzle their freshly squeezed unconcentrated juice, and some organic Kale, until sooner or later they KNOW, nature told them, they think. They no longer really require to see, and things are no longer hidden (barring being physically hidden), not admitted, or not accepted.

This defunct nucleus was the first laboratory of the Shell oil company, my mind rolled for a second, I came back round. The shell oil company. How did I wind up standing where i'm standing? I was overwhelmed, a neutral and grey kind. Not positive, but containing far too much peculiarity to be negative. The chuffing Shell oil company. It dawned on me in peak bloom what a perfect place this could be for the heartbeat of the 'OCCUPY' movement to seed from. Of all the places to plant some humanity, to grow roots watered with love, to spread out, touch, radiate, to encourage very different FEELINGS and let people know that they needn't suffer sore shoulders. A splendid tonic of rehydration. Emanating from the very same place that the 85% of the (55%) oil that is injected into the puddles was manufactured.

As I stared at the broken test tubes and window panels, and may I add that the damage was more minimal than I had imagined, a figure scooted past in the corridor and continued on. I walked back to the corridor and looked out left to see the grey ponytail bobbing toward me:

"Who was that? the key man enquired

"I have no idea, did he not saying anything to you?"

"NO! He just shot past, I was in the store room"

What should we do? I asked.

"We will have to follow him"

He scampered back to the main door and bolted it closed, so as to not let anyone else enter the labs while we went to investigate.

"It is probably someone who lives here" I reassured him.

"Maybe so, but its difficult to know who you can trust in here right now. There are a minority of people stealing and breaking things throughout the whole building, thats why we have had to lock the labs off in this way, the damage you just saw in there was done on the first day by activists who believed themselves to be sticking it to the proverbial man, but all they have done is make it harder for us to be here. There is damage to a particularly delicate part of the building upstairs, and there are barely any copper pipes left, people are gutting the building for profit and selling for personal gain"

I was aware of this activity, and felt strongly against it, it was not our building and it seemed to me, as it seemed to most people I had chatted with, that in order to remain there, we would have to respect it and keep it in the state that we found it. Surely that is one of the basic principles of squatting. This kind of negligence seemed to contradict the loose base principles that I felt the 'Occupy' movement stood for. After all, we were here to demonstrate, first and foremost, against the more severe and controlling strands of capitalism. The fact that some of our fellow activists were acting with such a disrespect for our integrity and with such selfishness, truly disconcerted me. Its not as though they were selling the pipes to raise money for resources for the community as a whole, something which would still have been unacceptable, but must be acknowledged as being far more understandable. The thought of where the money was going made me angry. I walked side by side with the ponytailed man, in deep thought. As we turned the corner I spoke:

"My name is Ben by the way."

"John, pleasure to meet you Ben."

We took a set of stairs towards the rear of the building, and clambered up to the next floor.

"Its hard to know where to start. He could be anywhere" John stated.

"Well you walk around this floor and I will head up to the next one, see if we can't spot him?" I proposed.

"Ok good plan."

I was getting used to the structure of the building in terms of navigating around it. If the office block side of the building was creepy, this side was straight out of a horror film. Rows and rows of labs and old cobwebbed equipment, special test rooms, do not enter, DANGER, DANGER. Goggles, old plastic goggles hanging where they had last being placed by unknown hands, who knows how many years ago:

"Hello.......Hello"

After 5 minutes of parading round the whole floor and shouting hello at the top end of my voice it became clear that our friend was not on this floor, and certainly not wanting to be seen. I wandered back towards the stair cases, shouting hello a little quieter:

"Hello, anyone here?"

Footsteps rising, I looked down over the bannister to see John rising.

"No luck?"

"Not up here" I answered.

"No nothing down here either."

"Let's look on the top floor together" I suggested. "Unless he slipped back past us he must be up there, and you locked the door downstairs."

"Yes but there are one or two ways that you can get out from the inside, I have tried to lock everything off the best I can, but some of the doors are locked from the outside with wood jammed behind them. He could have moved the block from inside and got out. I don't have enough padlocks to lock off every door. My betting is he got whatever he was after quickly and got out of here on the first floor. Lets have quick look upstairs anyway though."

I felt a bolt of anger dash through me. How could someone that was living here show such greed and lack of care for what we were trying to achieve. It felt so ignorant. I wanted to believe it was an outsider who had snuck in. We looked around the top floor briefly. Not a peep. Our man was long gone. I looked once more at John, he looked tired. I really felt for him. He seemed to be putting in so much effort and he was getting it thrown right back in his face. I didn't want to accept it but I thought to myself that this was maybe something that I might have to get used to in this place until things started becoming a little more structured.

Me and John began acquainting ourselves. He told me of his youth, growing up in L.A, going to watch 'The Doors'. Wow. Interesting man. I gave him a hand reinforcing a few of the locking devices on the doorways he thought needed it, and gave him an ear to vent some frustration. Boy he needed it. Down in the basement we found the place our friend had exited, copper in tow, we presumed. As we wandered back in the direction of the exit I became intrigued once more:

"You said as we started coming up here that damage had been done to a very delicate area of the building. What did you mean? I questioned.

"Oh the stained glass windows further across. They contain much symbolism and the one on the 2nd floor contains the symbol of the 'Illuminati', so some clever soul decided it apparent to run up and headbutt it, you know, sticking it to the man and all…mmmmmm"

"May I see?"

"Ok, quickly."

We headed over to the windows. They truly were a sight to behold. The was one situated on each floor, at the rear of each stairwell. Each individually crafted.

Birds, the emblem of the shell company, all sorts of symbolisms, all original to the building. It really made you think. And there, sure enough, on the 2nd floor, amongst a plethora of other well detailed images, and forehead sized crack through the middle of the pyramid and eye that sits on every U.S bank note.

A little while after Jon showed me the windows, there was a press story about them, and it wasn't about how interesting they were, no! It turned out that one of the original demonstrators who had been asked to leave the building, for reasons undisclosed to me, had been allowed back in one day just before my arrival. He took pictures of the damaged windows. the fact of this matter leaked around the inhabit ants of the building, and was another reason why it was decided that the area should be locked. In his frustration he decided to take the pictures to the newspaper, who of course decided to write a big NEGATIVE, out of proportion, article about 'Occupy' and all the happenings in the shell building. Amazing what people will do for, what they think is, revenge. Amazing the shit that people publish to sell a story, amazing what people believe, incredible the affect it has. A finger up the arse of slander, and two up its nostrils and into the spot in its mind that cunningly persuades or dissuades us, dependant on its agenda. The filthy lawyer. What about the POSITIVES? huh?

Needless to say that the story opened up another tin of worms that would require our sifting through, should we still wish for our quest to brighten.

✶✶✶✶✶✶✶

Amsterdam! Oh I love you Amsterdam. It's a knowing. The observation of Paris's romance are noted so oft, but Amsterdam, mmmmmm, pristine but human, open and unassuming, mindful and beautiful. Riding leisurely along canals, drawn by moonlight, surrounded by splendid architecture, well built, with history, culture, a story, a million romantic stories, millions more. House boats decorated with a subtle tentative touch, vast, beautifully maintained parks, proud without arrogance, stylish in sleep, quaint despite magnitude. I dare you to find a more tranquil city that contains the same depth of character and energy on this planet, there cannot be many to compare. Bike parks that are so thick with bikes they look like swarms and swarms of bees tightly packed into undersized hives. If I left a bike in the middle of one of them I would never possess the brain capacity to find it again, for sure, but these guys and gals do, they do have that capacity. The bike lane is a road, and its the main road, cable cars buzz around respectfully, the odd car and taxi pass through, but this is the territory of the bike, the push bike, the two wheeler, the tandem, the lay-z boy bike, and oh how the city benefits from this fact. The air clearer, the noise pollution turned down, dopamine releases on the constant, and bike spokes spinning fin splendour. Amsterdam, Amsterdam, Amssshhhhhterdam!

I met a girl called Flora in a square just down from the Beurspliene, a sweet local girl with an honest warmth that helped me to feel at home just after my arrival to the city. She took me for coffee at her favourite shop, showed me some lesser known spots of beauty (there are many), I met her family, she lived in a little residential area of the city, full of beautifully crafted houses horseshoeing gently about an old well maintained school building. The kind of place where you think 'it must be wonderful to be a child growing up here'. She tried to help me find a sleeping bag for the shell building, problem was I needed 5, it was bitter and that word suits too well. She lent me another. Flora was the prime example of how I would like to treat a new entry to England. With understanding, compassion, and care. She allowed me to enjoy my wonder by pointing me in the direction of it. I remember well,after we shopped, she had her bike. I was on foot as I had not purchased my bike yet. She told me to hop on the shelf at the back. After a couple of minutes of giggles and failure I was sat there on the back riding through the streets of Amsterdam. I had seen girls riding along like this, legs crossed, hands clenched, with blissful serene looks on their faces, and now I understood why. I crossed my legs, in-wove my hands, smiled and soaked. I was the princess for some minutes. Balance. The night after I managed to buy an old bike from a friend, I contacted Flora and asked if she wanted to take a cycle. We met in the dark. As she pulled up I saw she had a back pack. It was a cold night. We spun our way along the canals, the wind biting our faces hard. Eventually we pulled up by the edge of the water and sat with our legs dangled down towards it. She pulled out snacks and a flask of warm Chocomel (hot chocolate). She explained to me how 'if I fell in I would probably go into shock and most certainly die'. This reassured me, as the Chocomel raised a toast to our insides. On the cycle back we passed the zoo. Flora told me a couple of stories about how her old school friends used to jump the fence at night and go and see the animals. She said she had always wanted to but never dared:

"Let's do it now." I suggested.

"No."

It took us probably 10 minutes to go through the logistics, but once we were over the railing we scampered like ninjas across the immediate lawn, as we came around the corner we found the penguins. Wow. They looked so peaceful. Like they'd just eaten dinner a couple of hours back and were just winding down and thinking about making a move for bed in the not so distant, some stood together, some pottered quietly, minding their own business. We felt liberated. We stood and quietly observed for a minute or two before we heard movement in the darkness behind us. We looked at each other and without a word scampered back to the far end of the railings before climbing back over. We stood laughing and catching our breath for a while, before looking over and seeing a security guard shining a torch at the exact area in which we had been standing a minute previous. We jumped on our bikes and pedalled off with contented grins on our faces. Thankyou for those memories Flora De Vries, good to meets ya, but thank you most of all for being human. Bless you for that.

****

Alex's room was too big, I only stayed in it for two nights before deciding I needed something smaller. If I was going to find a way to keep warm I needed a smaller space to heat, logically. One morning I searched the building high and low looking for unoccupied space that gave me a good feeling, Feng Shui and all that jazz. I was trying to plant my seed, to grow myself out of, to take root, to feel comfortable, basic requirements, in order that I may grow and bloom out. The task of finding this space was tougher than I imagined. The building had lots of empty room, and many of them gave me the instinctive peace I was chasing, but not so many remained that didn't have someones name on. Who were these people. People seemed to be leaving and arriving at the building all the time. It seemed that on the first day people occupied a room, and some of those people were still there, but a lot weren't, just a room, with maybe nothing in, or maybe a shabby mattress, or maybe a plastic bag. Were they returning? Sometimes newcomers would move into what seemed to be an empty room, just a name on the door, and then a few days later the person who wrote on the door would return and the newcomer would have to relocate again. Had they been at the beurspliene campsite? At work? Away? No one knew, you could ask and nobody would know who they were, until they re-emerged again and a face was recognised.

   The communication was awful. Was not a list of people who were living in the building taken in the first day? Or something. Even as a basic fire safety measure. Ok so we don't want to govern this place in a rigid way but we have to have some degree of organisation, an outline of structure, if only to develop a collective understanding. It may take us a lot longer to get on the same page but at least lets keep our heads in the same book. It dawned on me that the (seemingly) almost complete absence of organisation and degree of looseness in the first two or 3 days of the building being squatted, may have led to an explosive cataclysm of misunderstanding and disorganisation. It was dripping down the walls. Too many people were subjectively deciding what was right and ok for them, rather than objectively deciding what was right and ok for our sustainability and for the people around them. Whatever the mission was, and no matter how many different species of positive missions were to be born out of this frustration we felt, it should be instinctively clear that the ground is going to need a patient levelling before foundations can be sustainably placed. Mindful, fair, conscientious, well organised and strongly communicated plans may be imperative at this point, or else chaos may decide to create cracks in the building walls and pull it apart into fragmented desolate islands. It's hard to work out kinks in yourself and around you when you are not befitted with enough information. COMMUNICATION.

   After a little while I found an smaller, unoccupied room on the 2nd floor. The door had no writing on but would not close properly, there was a problem with the hinge. I borrowed some tools from Gorka and managed to take off the part that was causing the problems, the door closed. I borrowed some graffiti and sprayed 'OCCUPY BEN' on it. A much lighter feeling scurried through me. I went into town and found a market stall with door locks, bought two, and returned home to assemble them. I put one on my new bedroom door and one on Alex's room. Alex had left the country but said he intended to return, I would hold his room open for him. If any newcomers were looking for a place to stay they could use his room and feel safe in there, and I would start turning the room into a venue/performance room in his absence. Me and Lucas had already discussed the idea of putting on a conscious evening of poetry readings and music, which was in the pipeline. I took all my bags and bedding and ventured down to my new room. The door was to the right. I set up my bed along the front left wall, Head to left wall, feet towards the front of the building. I placed my suitcases up against the wall, shut the door, twisted the lock, and sat in the middle of the room for a few minutes. Aaaaahhhhhh, it felt good, safe. I thought about how I might try and keep a little warmer at night and wondered what else I could do to create a little more comfort. Strolling through another one of Amsterdam's beautiful street markets, I bought myself a cheap pair of red stretchy jeans, some thick foam matting from the army store, a duvet to wrap around my sleeping bags, a new hat, a boiling pan, and an abundance of candles. As I returned to the front yard I re-noticed the huge pile of bricks and stone to the far corner. They gave me an idea. I felt momentarily inspired. I spent the next hour dragging little piles of brick and stone up to my new room. After a while I had plenty. I constructed 5 heaters, There was one in each of the four corners of the room (the one in the corner where my bed lay was set across a little in the position of a bedside table), and one in the very centre of the room. I made them by laying 4 or 5 bricks to form a foundation, which essentially made a larger square. I then added a circulation of brick on top, leaving a cavity in the middle. In each cavity I placed 3 tea lights and lit them. Finally I placed a square, 2 inch thick, slab of stone over the bricks, like a roof, and waited. Sure enough,after 15 minutes or so the top slabs of rock started warming up, insulating, and radiating heat. What else could I do to get it a little warmer? I remembered seeing some small metal holed sheets down in the basement, kind of like grill trays or something. I went to investigate and picked up five in the right size, a slightly larger one, and a number of pieces of 6x6 inch, yellow and blue cloth floor tiles. I took off each roof slap of the tea light heaters and placed a metal holed sheet on top of the walls, before replacing the stone slabs back on top, with the metal acting as the cheese slice of the square burger, if you will.

Next I placed my incense tray on one of the yellow fabric floor tiles and put it next to the tea light heater in the centre of the room, I placed a blue one next to it and carried on placing the tiles, in alternating colours, until the heater was surrounded. I then placed another layer of tiles to the outer side of the previous layer, as if it was growing and expanding out from the centre, I left the four corners of the outer layer untiled (see diagram). This was all quite instinctive behaviour for me, and has since influenced me towards wanting to develop deeper insights into the significance of ceremony and of geometric shapes, such a the flower of life etc. I put candles all along the shelf, around all the walls, and all around the rim of the centre tea light heater. When lighting these latter tea-lights, I used a lighter for the first on,e and then used it to light the 2nd one, then the 2nd to light the 3rd, the 3rd to light the 4th, and so on, until they were all lit. I thought about how they were all connected to each other more strongly now. It felt like I was a child playing once more with my innocent imagination. I thought about families, friends, dominos and russian dolls. Lighting the Nag Champa I checked on the tea light heaters. The tea lights in their hollow were giving energy to the metal sheets and the stone, the metal was in turn passing heat through to the stone slabs as well. Go team! I thought to myself that the metal just needed some encouragement from the tea light to get motivated for its mission to heat the stone slab, I wondered whether this explained something in a human context. Was there some analogy to be drawn about how we could get things moving in a more positive direction, with each others help?

The stones were now really nice and hot. I sat on one of them with crossed legs. The heat travelled up my back and began to warm me through, one chakra at a time. It dawned on me how much I needed it. I was so satisfied and proud of my friend the tea light, I knew he was powerful, but the amount of work he does for his size is immense. I took a couple of his brothers and sisters and placed them in front of me before hovering my toes over them. Mmmmmmmmmm. I took the remaining, larger, metal sheet, curved its edges round to raise it a little, placed 5 tea lights underneath it in the shape of a pentagon, and put my boiling pan on top of it, before tipping in half a carton of Chocomel. To my absolute pleasure this trick worked too, and within 10 minutes I was sipping on hot Chocomel, as well as sitting like a buddha wannabe on my warm stony perch. For the first time in a few days I felt warm enough. My room was in place, the fear of bedtime no longer loomed over me, it now almost excited me in fact. The idea of waking up in the morning seemed more bearable. My mind was cleaner. I felt for the first time as though my mind could perhaps now comfortably move out of survival mode and start applying itself to something more vast. I was lucky enough to have a little money: For food, a comfy bed, and heat. I had obtained my basics and a little symmetry. I felt very in tune and ready, ready for whatever was in store.

A few days passed and things seemed ok. I walked out one morning to a crowd of people. They were sitting on the steps, standing in groups, looking highly spirited. Bikes flocking to, bikes spinning back, ideas, suggestions. A small group were stood eyeing up the entrance. The outer door of the entrance was of glass, a slide door that was old and in need of a great deal of lubrication, it had become pretty stuck to the point where the larger framed human specimens were having difficulty squeezing in and out. In the crowd stood John, Gorka, and a couple of other familiar faces. They were about to fit a new door. Some of the more student based occupiers were bringing fellow students and friends around the building and trying to encourage interest in projects, and generally get involved with the cultivation of the place. Everyone seemed excited by the prospects. Out in the yard was Dirk (the man who squatted the building and chief suspect of the copper raids), trying in earnest to move heavy stones over to help construct a toilet area. He looked to be struggling. I decided to go and see if he needed a hand, I had spoken to him for 5 minutes in the front doorway previously, whilst smoking a cigarette. He had seemed very chilled and quite friendly, he asked where I was from and showed a little interest, and yet since then, all I had heard about him was in reference to him standing accused of the copper disappearances:

"Hows it going man?" I asked.

"Ah" he splurged, sweeping his brow, "I'm ok, its heavy work"

"I will give you a hand"

He seemed pleased, maybe a little surprised. It occurred to me later that perhaps he was doing the work on his own because no-one else would go and help him, people were perhaps choosing to not help him, he was in the proverbial doghouse, though he was certainly not in everyones doghouse. What I saw in that moment was a man who knew what people were thinking about him, trying to make an effort, and guilty or not, there is at least something that has to be admired in that. We began putting the tent in place, and holding down the ropes with the stones we dragged across from a stone pile towards the front of the yard. The yard was perhaps as big a 2 or 3 fully sized football pitches. After a few sporadic blasts of small talk I managed to diplomatically weave in a chance to talk about the accusations against him. He told me that a group of them took some copper on the first day, he said he had admitted that, a very modest amount, and that he had had nothing to do with the continuation of the copper disappearances. I am not saying I believed him and I am not saying I didn't, but together we were trying to construct a toilet for everyone.

A new door was fitted, with a lock. Positive vibes put out, can we change the minds of the public? Thought of the day: Everyone will see the sickness in the others before they catch glimpse of the sickness in themselves. We need to double check to see if the sickness we see in the other is really there, because if after all it isn't, then we may have been looking in the mirror. Let us not be ruled by our perception, and not too proud to change it.

****

"Mic check, MIC CHECK a one a two-a"

I put out my cigarette and scampered to the general assembly room, it seemed evident that this would be a crucial one. 8 candles, 13 candles, 21? Who knows, much lighter than the first time though. About 20 people. Where's the rest. Who knows, shall we wait a while, chatter chatter, wait, wait, where? Who? Not coming? Who isn't. Dirk was in the room, lots of people weren't. The general assembly (?) commenced. It wasn't right though. I stuck around for it. It lasted about 10 minutes, no one knew what was going on, Lucas tried a few points of interest, then it ended. Where were the others? In a pocket somewhere for sure, hell, maybe there was 10 meetings happening right now, all positive they had the answers, reinforcing this belief by surrounding themselves with all of those sharing similar agendas, similar discriminations. Great stuff guys. Pockets in pockets, fight each other, good job, I think not. I walked upstairs and headed to the place I thought they would be, and there they were, a group of them. These were passionate people, these were good people, but had they just skipped a general assembly with everyone, because they didn't like one guy there? The Dirk haters? and now they were planning behind the backs of everyone not invited to the room, in a little microcosm, with no power in truth, just the over zealous belief that they could take 'control', while all possible cohesion was being thwarted by this elitist idea. Animal Farm. Oink oink piggies. Ok, so we are here to demonstrate against the elite and we will do that by forming an elite. Good plan Stan. In fairness to a couple of the people in the room, as well as seeming not to be rolling venom around their mouths like the others, they were not living full time at the shell building either, so were perhaps a little out of touch with my perception of the situation. Also, in fairness to the rest, they were fed up, fed up with things disappearing, being broken. They had decided to go to war, but they were at war with themselves, they were letting their negative emotions control them. They would expend all their energy on trying to get rid of certain people from the building, for reasons not discluding personal vendetta, and it sucked them dry. Perhaps they had fair points in part, but we were living inside of chaos, we had no structure, and strange things happen in chaos, it can make people act out of sorts, some understanding and forgiveness needs to be implemented there. I think to Gorka and the 'no bullshit' approach of getting on with things and I wonder what that room full of great minds could have fathomed should they have been able to find a way to not let such little sticks cog their systems. There were also issues with a guy called Hugo who was deemed as being "violent", there seemed to be some kind of effort to oust him as well.

****

Another day unrolled, the plants towered another half millimetre taller, the penguins in the zoo awoke in a dream states wondering how they might 'play' today. My Chocomel began to bubble and send lapping waves of its rich odour to my icy nostrils, my breath skipping across the room on tiny thin ice sheets. I sat in my duvet and sleeping bag cocoon with my hat pulled way down over my ears. More bearable, so much more bearable. I took a walk down to the front hall and front door to see if anyone like John or Gorka were around, and whether they had jobs to do that I might help with, but I couldn't see them, just a few younger people with whom I was not very well acquainted. They looked like they had had a cold night, and were trying to wake up their bodies with hot tea. I thought I might pay a visit to the internal yard.

   The yard was one of a few internal yards, but this one, for whatever reason, had become 'the' yard. It had that POTENTIAL. It was a large rectangular shape, concealed and unseen in the middle of the building. The secret yard-en. It was concealed inside four walls that ran up high, all the way to the buildings flattened roof. There were a few randomly placed seats towards the middle, alongside a steel drum with its top cut off, out of the drum usually roared a fire. Under darkness the flames reflected in the windows that ran the full perimeter of the walls, separating the inside corridors from the bitter winter air, giving the impression that it was warming everything through. It wasn't, but when you gathered around the drum, heat certainly was to be had. A few sporadic efforts were made to make food on the drum fire, on each occasion making enough food to feed maybe one third of the habitants. To be honest you would be very lucky to see one third of the occupants in one place at one time, at any time, so the food would most often suffice, not that I was always there to know. The deck of the yard was of a standard concrete, strewn with little pieces of straw pulled around by the scraping feet of the two chickens that lived freely.

   The chickens could best be found parading the surroundings of their little house in a morning yard visit. This was my favourite time for a yard visit. Especially under a bright clear winter sky, with the gently glowing aftermath of the firedrum. You could often find yourself on your own, with time for a little reflection, at this time of day. There was something inspiring about it, raw potential I think, all coiled up inside a fresh day.

   As I walked out onto the yard I saw Mascha, sat on her own next to the drum:

"Hey, you ok?" I said softly.

"Yeah, you? She replied.

We chatted in a relaxed manner for a little while. I knew she had been there since the very start and knew most people quite well. I conveyed some of my ideas to her, maybe wondering, and probably hoping, that it would give them more hope of manifestation. She seemed to be in concurrence with what I was saying, maybe it was all in my head, but she even seemed refreshed by my words. I felt positive. I looked at the sky, feeling anything was possible, good times were ahead. As I gazed up high at a beautiful, crystal blue, Amsterdam sky, I noticed, in my periphery, a ladder that was rising up all the way up to the roof of the building:

"Has anyone been up there yet", I half joked.

"Ha, no I don't think so", Mascha returned.

I paused in thought for few seconds........1......2...3..........4...............5...6..7!

"I'm gonna climb it", I declared.

"No...Seriously?....Are you sure?....I don't know if thats a good idea"

   I was already on the ascent. Slowly, slower, slow and slowest, one rung at a time, grip tight. If I lost grip? If there are l-o-o-s-e screws and bolts?
   Then I fall! And though its not ridiculously high, its high enough, if I fall? Well....
   But to reach the top would be so liberating for sure. It may not mean much to anyone else, just a few unrequired social points, 'he who dared', no, this was for me. Some kind of proof and manifest confirmation that if we dare, we can achieve what we desire, if we believe, then we really really can. At first it was easy, low fear, higher tempo, as I reached the middle the mix changed:

```
P          S
U          P
           E
S          E
E          D
D
I          S
L          L
S          U
           M
R          P
A          S
E
F          D
           O
           W
           N
```

I was so determined to break through. To achieve. Why did I feel so strongly for it? Yes it must have been personal confirmation. A symbol of 'Occupy'? The further we go, the harder it will become? The higher the risks, the more resistance we would meet? The more ruthless gravity would be? Was greed a rusty screw at the top of the ladder? Tolerating our climb to a certain level, before interpreting us as intruders and a threat, moving itself and its assets over to another screw, and dislodging its former self just as we were to reach the summit, sending us cascading down to meet our end? Our makers? Our higher selves?

Slowly, slower, slow and slowest, I was nearing the top, literally shaking, but my grip was good, I was determined. Mascha watched on from the the yard, I felt for her, she was more or less out of control of my fate, well, perhaps not, I'm sure her wishes were with my success, and so maybe she was affecting somewhat my fate, but if my hand were to slip, if other influences were to make my vice grip relent, what then? She would be the sole witness, oh what a burden that would be:

"Erm…..shit, guys, Ben has just fallen from the top of the ladder up to the roof of the building, someone got told that their profit margins are down, and we are in part responsible, they're livid, they contrived to make him lose his grip, what are we gonna do? He's out in the yard in a crumpled pile"

5 more rungs, 4 more, 3, that weird semi scared/semi excited sensation that you used to get all the time when you were a kid, like you need to piss, and all the bitter sweetness of it is building up all around your bladder, and a tiny bit squirts out. 2 to go, man, last one, and slide, It felt like it took an age to crawl onto the top of where the rungs curled round to attach to the roof, but crawl I did. Marsha must have seen my body disappear in gradual, first my head, upper body, midriff, legs, feet, SAFETY!

I can't properly describe the feeling:

'Sings the quenched consciousness,
with no sleight of mouth'

Maybe this was the peak of my own personal belief in the 'OCCUPY' cause. I stood up and peeked back down over into the courtyard to see Mascha, cutting a relieved figure. In retrospect, perhaps I had started playing games in my own head to help me believe, to give me my faith, but in those brief moments it mattered little, I had my faith:

"Woooooo" I exhaled.

"Ha, I will come up", she yelled.

She walked out of the yard and opted for the stairs. I toddled slowly over to the front end of the building, pulled out a smoke and embraced the view I was withholding. Full up on thoughts of unlimited possibility and divine freedom, I glanced out over one of this worlds most beautiful cities. The canals glistened under the trying frost of early winter. The delicate wind swept across my face and through my hair to congratulate my own subjective, relatively insignificant stunt. I looked down at the barren garden/yard area in front of the building. I could see it all now in my minds eye. The community garden, benches dotted around. An old couple enjoying a nice warm cup of tea they have bought from our cafe, admiring the daffodils. A group of children dislodging chunks of wood chip as they swing back and forth in the newly built play park. A group of students arriving for a meeting in room 5, to discuss further, the recent matters at hand. A contented new guitarist walking back to the shuttle ferry with 4 new chords learnt from her donation based lesson. Ah, wow, the opportunities would be abundant, the energy electric, the love warm, the faith restored.

I heard a door open and out onto the roof waltzed Mascha and Lucas:

"I hear you got up here by the route less travelled" smiled Lucas.

"Ha, yeah, you know what, this is still such a wonderful opportunity, there is still a difference to be made"

"Your'e right", they agreed.

We laughed, joked, discussed, imagined and breathed down to the pits of our abdomens, some deep sense of liberation, some great sense of purpose. It smelt so good, so so good.

****

The next afternoon I walked out of my room to head out. As I locked up I realised I had a new neighbour. A sweet young girl was painting the name 'Didi' on her door with a flowery font. I had been introduced to her the night previous by Gorka, who lived just round the corner from me, and she had decided to move into our neck of the woods. I told her I was going for food and she joined me. As we chatted she disclosed to me that she was from 'Jordan'. She had decided to leave her country because of the unrest, and had somehow emerged in Amsterdam, joined 'occupy', and was living away from home, in a squat, for the first time. She was full of enthusiasm and ideas, and was keen to apply her energy towards some community projects. I thought about the beauty, the intricacy, and the chance that brings people from all walks of life to a place, in the hope they may manifest a common goal, whatever that goal might be, in our case, a goal to try and do a part for a community we hadn't quite fathomed just yet, such is the diversity that leads us to that common goal. A want to do something with and for your fellow man, for posterity. We may seem a long distance apart, in terms of location, upbringing, custom, preference, or understanding, but, are not dimensions that influence us on this plane full of beautiful unseen twists and tricks and shortcuts. I think we are always a lot closer than we might sometimes believe, if we want to be, or even if we don't. Oneness. The font. The godhead, filtering down through the dimensions and creating wonderful intricately woven table cloths, for form. Cosmic attraction? Fate? Destiny? Love? Little loving radars watching our steps and helping us to the new checkpoints when we require. For learning, for understanding, for expansion, both in and out.

I popped out again that night to pick up some shopping, there was no scheduled general assembly that night, but I believe an emergency one may have been called just after I left for the city. When I arrived back two hours later I was surprised to find that the doors had been smeared with coloured paints. I was utterly confused as the housemate on the door let me on through.

"Whats happened here" I enquired

"Dirk" came the answer. "a group of people threw him out for the stealing of the copper pipes and he went crazy, throwing paint at the door and rubbing it in, yelling and screaming, and reportedly declaring "that the revolution could not unfold without him"

I couldn't believe it, I didn't know what to think. I really didn't. I was on the fence, I couldn't really not be. I didn't have the information to form a true enough opinion, I wished for a second that I had been there from the very start, maybe then I could see clearer. I didn't know exactly how he had been thrown out. I hoped it wasn't too brutal. He did not seem like a violent man. I wondered how embarrassing the situation may have been for him.

Days kept turning and they kept filling me with mixed emotions. The media seemed to be around quite a lot, hunting a story, some people spoke to them I guess. The media portrayal of us was ugly and totally ill founded, barring those sporadic moments of individual idiocy of course. They didn't want any stories about what plans we had, just drama, ah, you know it, never trust a story, but people do, or it puts that reasonable (unreasonable) doubt in a cell of a mind. In my head one of the main ways in which we would get 'community projects' kicked off would be to show the general public that we were there to happily and lovingly help facilitate their needs too. I proposed an information stand in the front yard so passing people would be encouraged to come and chat with us. Maybe we could give out some free tea to warm the cockles and have some music playing, live or other, you know, something nice and informal. The problem with bad media is that it makes the chance of people stopping by for an open chat a little more unlikely. Once people picked up a paper and read about this place where all people do is ingest drugs, vandalize, and steal piping, they do not want to come near the place. So I would like to spend a moment flicking some more fingers at the reporters who wrote such stories. Standing weakly behind the horrendous justification that you are "only doing your job", it is my belief that you conduct a vile deed, just as your conscience tells you you do, halting human progression (and don't forget your human) for your measly salary.

Every time I met a local in the city they would be aware of what a "freak show" it was over at the shell building. The truth is that these things are always sensationalised, they are never in context. There were professors in there, art therapists, teachers, forward thinking students, learned people, doing positive things and infiltrating positive ideas, but drama is what keeps the papers in print, so drama is chased. A few of the squatters reacted very badly to this negative media and returned to the Beurspliene camp site. It was getting harder to keep going and remain positive but people kept coming up with new ideas, and new people would keep arriving and injecting new energy in and around those of us that were in fear of getting drained. John however, was completely drained, he said to me that maybe he needed a few nights away to get clean and refresh, he had a friend nearby. I told him that I thought it to be a wonderful idea. I came up with a personal plan to try and counteract the negative energy around me. The plan was simple, anytime I see a negative, I should try to take at least two positive actions.

One day I wandered out of the building to find people standing around complaining that someone had been over in the night and smashed a window. One of the lads with an agenda walked out in a huff and kept pointing at the window as he walked off site, disgraced by it, in fact, seemingly disgraced by anyone and anything. He said something rather rude to someone, I shouted after him "Why don't you do something about it then" before picking up a dustpan and brush from the hallway and cleaning up the glass. It didn't take long at all, I walked over and put it in the bin as a group of people just watched me. I then began trying to construct the outlines of a recycling area, and made a sign for the front fence reading 'OCCUPY COMMUNITY PROJECTS'. I thought for a little while about how there can be a natural flow to everything if you choose to see it. The day before the windows were broken Gorka invited round a graffiti artist to paint up some boards he had. It occurred to me that the boards were the exact right size to cover up the broken window, why hell, we could have artwork all across the bottom of the building if we liked. We could get children from schools to come and paint the bricks, and take guitar lessons if they choose, or spanish classes, whatever. I realised that the media coverage we had had was going to decrease the likelihood of any children being allowed over here, for fear of their safety, for the time being at least, until we could paint a happier picture for the media to stick on with their pritstick, and sprinkle on their shiny sparkles. The artwork boarding never manifested for whatever reason but the idea was important in making me realise that it is not impossible to carve a negative into a positive. One step back, two steps forward. I like that, we hear it the other way round far too much.

Me and Lucas finally set a date for our music and spoken word night 'Powered by tea-lights'. We invited everyone from the building, and friends, and friends of friends from outside. We held the night in Alex's room as planned. Lucas shared some spoken work, I shared some music, and a spanish chap played some music also. As the name of the night would suggest, we covered the whole room with tea-lights and it was beautiful. People sprawled around the floor, some sat on chairs. Cold, weary bodies gathered together in warmth, in a peaceful, sharing environment of song and word. Everyone had a nice evening and it turned out just as well as we could have hoped.

✸✸✸✸✸✸✸

It could have been Thursday, or one of the others. Who cares. Dirk returned anyway, with his friends, and occupied the other side of the building. Of course he did. That wasn't a surprise. Well, most of the original activists seemed pretty unshaken by this, many people there always got on with Dirk. Most of the people who had him ousted had left the building now anyway and were living back down at Beurspliene. I had already started paying way more attention to Beurspliene, making many more visits down there. It was not a happy place, looking back it was like a caught fish wriggling on deck, to suffocate, to die. The COUGH camp, shit, some, if not most of those people had been living on that little square, in their tents, in the freezing cold, for weeks and weeks. I am sure that each major and each minor note on the musical scale could be heard (to an ear trained better than mine) from the coughs that grunted and whined down there. It was sad, so sad, did people really know why they were there? Were they waiting, waiting and waiting, for that something, that wasn't coming? The rumour mill was rife down there too, again, COMMUNICATION, it was broken, jaded, deluded, schizophrenic. Dirk deserved no second chance in their eyes. They would oft gather in the little information tent and spout nought but negativity. They were beautiful people, they could just take no more, they could not see straight, things were ah-yah-hhmmm-a a little scattered. Rumours were out of control, the amplifier was turned up to 11. Bless them, every one of them. A press statement was released from the camp to state that Occupy no longer has anything to do with the shell building, and they withdrew the name. This was disclaimer press in a way I guess, but there were still a lot of connections between the two sites and lots of people were still committed to working to get things back on track at shell. We would just get on with our efforts as usual. One thing that started to stand out strongly to me was just how much of a dream it must have been for the police. See, the dutch police and dutch people (in my opinion), don't often tend to be the sort of people to jump in straight away, the police may often wait until they are forced to intervene instead of diving in head first. All they had to do was wait, wait and watch, wait while we rip each others balls off, as we were, so to speak. We were like rabbits in our holes, almost without any supplies. And we would live on the other side of the building to each other, like squabbling siblings. They had both our entrances covered with their rifles cocked and their clear focused heads of concentration. I speak only in metaphor here and wish not to say that all the police were waiting to clear us out in a militant sense, I am positive there were individuals associated with the police who were extremely open and supportive of a positive occupation, and I personally encountered a number of police in the front yard who always contained respect in their manner of speech. My point mainly that we were eating our own balls, and they tasted terrible.

****

Friday night arrived and some folks started chatting of a club they were all thinking of heading to, I wanted to let go, let the hair down, and shake my little booty butt, but I couldn't. Lucas informed me that the neighbours, a sweet artist commune, would be heading round tomorrow to pick up some chairs they had stored down in our basement. He was concerned that no-one would be around first thing to help facilitate the move, as everyone was heading out.

"I'll meet them" I said, "I'm not heading out tonight anyway"

"Really, why not?"

"I just don't really feel like it, go ahead and enjoy"

I ascended the dark gloomy stairs once more, no doubt about it, they were getting gloomier, darker, a little more contorted with each climb. I went to my room and lit some incense, stoked the tea light heaters and fumbled for my writing pad. I began etching some notes that I wanted to bring up at the next general assembly. Just then there was a knock on the door, "come in" I said, and in walked Didi:

"Good evening" she said,

"Hey"

"You heading out tonight"

"Not tonight"

We chatted to catch up for a little while, talking , as was becoming more and more common, about a different example of one of the same problems we were all encountering. But as she continued I was delighted to learn that she had been spending some time with Hugo, yes Hugo, the violent one that was to be ousted with "immediate god damn effect", and guess what, she didn't find a bad word to say against him. This pleased me so. We wandered over to his room and spent a couple of hours sitting around smoking, laughing and drinking tea with some of the other Spanish, Hugo kept asking me if I needed a top up of brew, that terrible dangerous man.

The next morning the neighbours arrived early, I helped them stack and lift chairs for a couple of hours into their vans and it was very civil. One of the women gave me her number and reiterated the offer for us to use their computer facilities. May I also add that the chairs that the neighbours collected from the basement where being used, in part, by the residents (including myself) as furniture for our rooms. As soon as we found out that the chairs were to be collected, we did a whip around the building and managed to retrieve (with no objections from anyone), all of the them. As the neighbours left I sat in the foyer for a little while and contemplated.

Sunday, and I rose at sun up, and got a tram down to the market place, but brushed straight through most of it and sat in a cafe overlooking a canal. I carried on writing, as many ideas as I could fathom. There was a general assembly this afternoon. I wanted to try and get some points passed that I felt may help us start co-operating with one another better. I scribed and scribed. As I got back to the front yard I was greeted by Lucas and introduced to a very professional and an elegant 40ish year old French man named Hoda. There was an intense glare down from his black rimmed glasses. He had just arrived:

"I'm heading over to the artist commune to type up some notes I've just made that I want to get passed at general assembly in an hour" I proclaimed,

"Oh great" returned Lucas, "Maybe we will head over with you and bounce some ideas around"

"Great"

The artists were lovely and we felt welcome, they brought a pot of tea over too. I read off the ideas I had and Hoda typed them up into bullet points, we added as much as we could think before heading back over to shell. The turnout for the general assembly was not stupendous, that was no surprise, but there were plenty there. I pointed out the woofing programme (worldwide organisation of organic farms) to the group, most were familiar. I proposed that we all work (in our own way) towards the community for at least 20 hours a week (unsupervised), and in return would be rightful and justified in occupying a room in the building. Agreement with this would result in you been given a key to gain entrance to the building, we naturally decided amongst us that guests of residents would be signed in and there would be no admittance for guests after 10pm each night, without prior agreement from the group (requests for such agreement could be put to the community at general assembly's and decisions would be fair and as objective as possible, within each given context). I felt an importance for us to take a step back from firmly rigid, militant, black and white, restrictive rules. Circumstances change like outfits and seasons. 'Decisions at each point of "now". Everybody agreed unanimously, and the idea was passed. It was clear that everyone wanted to live in a friendly, safe environment and points were passed regarding these issues, as well as others. The final point that was passed was a very exciting one. It involved us taking a pad and encouraging everyone to write down various groups that could be formed so we could start our work. There were all sort of headings:

- Kitchen
- Cleaning
- Building
- Renewable energies
- Spokespeople (of various factions)
- Events organisation
- Legal team
- Gardening
- Fundraising
- Co-ordinators.......
............the list went on, everyone then signed up for the groups they had expertise and/or interest in, and there was more excitement around the room than I'd seen in any general assembly before:

"I'm a chef"

"I've been working with renewable energies for a couple of years"

"I'm a tomato lover"

"I am THE Mr Muscle"

People seemed to simply fall naturally and gracefully into their places. fffwwtt. fffwwtt. fffwwttt. We all agreed that we would meet in the front foyer at 10am every monday to friday (provisionally) and see what was to be done. It seemed to me as though things could fall naturally into place. Sure there would be disagreements. But with a little compromise? A wish crossed my mind for everyone in the building, sod it, everyone involved in Occupy Amsterdam, darn it, everyone in Amsterdam right 'now' with any kind of sympathising interest with our plastered cause, to be in the room right now. I imagined us all packed tightly together, smaller ones sitting on bigger ones shoulders, all buzzing with excitement deep inside our chests, up and down our spines, as we finally realised the amplitude of what we had the right to achieve. Together.
    I woke up and there were maybe 20 of us, our frilly facades just that tiny bit

too short to cover the hurt trickling from our belly buttons. Shrunken in the wash. I would not say that I was naive enough to consider myself 'Optimistic', but I certainly knew that there was not much more that I could have personally done. I slept well, and looked forward to seeing what tomorrow brought.

****

Monday morning, 10am, front foyer. 6 people. Surprised? No. Disappointed? Why aye. John was back though, with another wind. He had managed to stay over at a friends for a couple of nights, to freshen up. It was nice to see him. So why didn't more people show up, they weren't faking their interest when they were running around trying to get a pen to sign up for groups yesterday. I have no answer still to this day, my theory is that most of those people hadn't found that point of comfort. Dam it was hard to, where's the peace in a place like this? As I already mentioned, I was fortunate enough to have a small amount of travelling money with which I was able to buy a duvet, and I had the sleeping bag from Flora, my hat, my heaters, and yet I was still a little cold in the middle of the night. Some people certainly didn't have the luxury of two sheets. People were suffering for sure, the main theft in the building was bedding, people couldn't get enough of it. Literally. If you spend a whole night shivering through, would you feel alert and ready to go and start work in the morning, in a place that you were not even sure any more that you weren't going to be kicked out of any day soon? There was an agreement in place that said that we had a good month or so, up to the court date, but I think there may have been some kind of return agreement that the place would be looked after, naturally, and what with the media coverage, and the rumours, and the confusion! were they really fine with us being there? The 6 of us stood around for a little while, discussed, and found a few little jobs to do, but we didn't have much. Moods were not high. A young lad walked out of the building with a backpack on, headphones in, and straight past us, a chap called Stefan lost it:

"I can't stand for this any more, who are these people living here? Who are some of these people? Who the fuck are you?" He shouted after the kid.

The boy took his earphones out in shock:

"Me?" He muttered defensively.

"Yes you, who the fuck are you, why are you here?"

The boy said his name, looked terrified, seemed to think for a second, then continued walking away. I felt for the kid because I'm human, but I could feel Stefan's pain completely. There were so many people thinking they could just come and go as they pleased, at their leisure, without doing absolutely anything for anyone else. If was more of an ironic ignorance than intentional disregard, a self-centredness, an inconvenience, an outright shame. We were here to demonstrate, less and less of us were doing so. The workers v the hedonists, really? The carers v the non carers.

In retrospect I suppose I knew this was the beginning of the end, well, probably it was more severe than that. Faith was shot, through the heart, but you just didn't want to accept it, it killed way too many dreams, shut off all those teeming avenues of colossal opportunity. Get up one more time you thought, you were numb enough to it now anyway, whats the difference. Ride out one more wave, just one. The young child, hooked on gummy worms, rummaging frantic sticky fingers around an empty paper bag, unaccepting of the reality of his situation.

In the afternoon I headed over to the other side of the building, it wasn't the first time I'd visited since Dirk returned. Lucas and Masha were spending more and more time over there, it was important that we all got on, it was imperative. In a lot of ways the other side of the building started to show more signs of life. There were many more empty rooms over on that side, and therefore new arrivals began to occupy rooms over there. Faith can sometimes be a funny and fickle thing. It was coming in waves. New arrivals would always have that slightly naive but completely beautiful belief in the cause, not too dissimilar to how I had felt when I first arrived. Newcomers never quite have the insight, and insight is not always our friend in these situations. Newcomers injected positivity and gave you something to check your state of mind against. It's easy to get too zoomed in, and without knowing it, newcomers can pull you way way back out until you see the whole picture again.

'OH YEAH!' That tricky mind thats yours and mine.

Some new arrivals were even more inspiring than others. One English girl and her Italian boyfriend even used their own funds to buy a few things for the community. I believe they bought a generator and a few bits and pieces to help out with a controversial idea to open up a room to the rear of the building into a space to hold parties and after parties. As part of the idea a bar would be easily set up which would generate money which would be used for resources. I have to say I was sceptical, it didn't seem like the temptation some people needed, but although the idea was never brought to general assembly, most people seemed keen on the idea, and it began to manifest. I question now sometimes the true motivations behind the backing of this idea, were people looking for an escape? The idea also made me think on about Dirk. I remembered back to something I had forgotten about my second day at the building. I had wandered down to the basement to take a look, Dirk was down there fetching some wood. He kept talking about a big party that was to happen in there, it seemed like his big plan. Party a la Dirk. At the time I didn't question it so much, it seemed clear to me that he wanted to put on the party for everyone, kind of like a big housewarming, and when you think of it like that, what better way to meet people and rejoice in good spirits. The party/festival atmosphere situation is something that has been a custom for just about every civilisation of people, for millennia and millennia. Having such a vision didn't make him a bad guy, it didn't mean he didn't want other more sensible, less instantly gratifying dreams to take root. Maybe the mistake was thinking about a party as the first main priority. I speculate here, but as the man who technically got everyone into the building, I imagine that in the first couple of days some people may have looked to Dirk as a leader type character. Had this leader type character thought more thoroughly about what type of structure the community truly needed in order to sustain, instead of making the main priority a party, then who knows what may have materialised. I don't mean to suggest that it was Dirk's responsibility to implement a tighter structure, and if people did have too much confidence in his ability to lead then that is not his fault either, unless he demanded that role. I merely mean that a tighter (not black and white tight) and more efficient and mindful organisational structure needed to be embedded around the communities awakening values and morales from day one, and it just wasn't. Without it an ethereal mindset could not develop. The collective consciousness and the group mind had no expansion juice. I wished it did have juice, worm tea, phenomenal fertiliser. Imagine it, 'the non black and white tight ship'. I want on. Up anchor, raise the sails, windy and warm, away boys, away girls, away!

✶✶✶✶✶✶✶

The following day I arose late, I needed the extra few hours. I'm not really one of those lucky souls that can sleep for 6 hours and run the marathon, I'm an 8 or 9 type of guy (you know that probably means 10), anyway, whatever, I deserved it, I felt, or I told myself. I poured out some chocomel and wandered leisurely down to the front yard. It was a relatively fine day. The wind only muttered, the sun was neither happy nor sad. The dogs responsible for the dog poo's scampered playfully around. I ventured close towards them. As I span around to gaze upon our crumbling palace I noticed a young lad, who I had seen a couple of times in passing, approaching me. We had nodded towards each other and I'd given him the "hey man", but we were yet to truly converse:

"Hey man" I started,

"Hey"

"How are you?"

"Que. No entiendo"

He was Spanish, and spoke no english.

I was English, and spoke no Spanish.

We struggled for a couple of minutes to converse, with hand actions and pointless slow speech, to extremely limited success. It was not awkward, we both knew what was occurring, and we smiled and chuckled about it more than anything. Just as we both seemed to be losing a little patience with the situation and he was probably thinking 'goodbye' simultaneously to me running the pronunciation of 'adios' through my head, I noticed a football near the bike rack and headed straight for it.

"You play?"

"Ah sie"

I dragged the ball back under my feet and flicked it to him. Both our faces lit a little, I was back in the playground. We spread out to an instinctively decided distance and began, a little stiffly, passing the ball back and forth to one another. After about three passes we got guests. The two dogs wanted in and began chasing down the ball. We both began to laugh and a game of 'Doggy in the middle' ensued. We played for around 10 to 15 minutes and I was laughing from my belly more than I had done in a long time. We had found our connection, despite the restriction. I thought about the duality between how useful language is in conveying information and ideas, but how sometimes we can perhaps come to lean on it a little too heavily. 'Actions speak louder than words', out of context or not, It's true.

The Spanish boy smiled, made the hand action of tipping a cup into his mouth (I understood that one), and trotted off into the building. I smiled, held up my hand, and pronounced "adios" to the best of my ability. I looked down at the dogs as they panted up at me from around my feet, and suddenly remembered that I had bought them some dog food from the store the night previous. I went up to my room to fetch it before emptying it out in the middle of the yard. They dismantled it in seconds, the poor things, they looked like they needed it, that's why I had bought it in the first place. They needed more resources, their owners needed more resources, we all needed more resources. Don't mistake me, no one was starving, but you need enough 'Go juice' to go, and it didn't seem to me like many people were 'good to go'. My money was getting rather depleted too.

As I finished watching the dogs keeping nuzzling and licking at what was now only dried mud where the food had been sitting, I noticed a character in the periphery of my right eye. I turned to see a casually well dressed man in his early thirties heading my way. I didn't recognise him, he pulled off his shades:

"Hi there, i'm David, I heard about you guys down here, I'm back in town for a couple of weeks, I'm american but I used to live over here in Amsterdam for years. How are things?"

I shook his hand:

"Good to meet you David, I'm Ben, from Yorkshire, England, I've been living here for over a month now."

"Cool. How are things going over here, I've heard some of the press releases."

"hhhmmmm, yeah it could be better, but its certainly not as bad as what you might be led to believe"

"Ha, I know what the press are like man, you take everything with a pinch of salt."

"Agreed, do you wanna have a look around the building."

I showed him around to give him a feel of what it was like, and we ventured up onto the roof to take a look at the city from above, it looked so beautiful still. After we came down from the roof we went to my room, rolled something to smoke, and began to chat. Soon enough, who David was and his interest in the place became much clearer:

"I have not been here for a couple of years but back in the 90's I lived in 3 squats over here. Obviously this was before squatting was criminalised, but I sourced each one myself and co-ordinated how it would work. Me and a group of around 20 others lived in a building overlooking Vondelpark for about two years. You overlooked the park from my bedroom windows on the top floor. In exchange for living in the building everyone did the place up. Most of the people there were labourers. We also lived in two other places for over a year a piece"

His words excited me. I told him about the problems we were encountering here and told him a few of the reasons it seemed liked things weren't talking root. He agreed with me conclusively and stated the following things as musts when squatting a building.

• Respect. You need to show complete respect to the building from the second you enter it. Make phone calls to the power companies straight away and make them aware that you will be the bill payer indefinitely from that date onwards. Nothing should be broken and if it is, its gotta be fixed (This made me think again about the stained glass window. We needed to get the funds together to have it repaired asap).
• The very first people who enter the building should have brainstormed meticulously and considered everything that they can conceivably muster. There should be huge trust between these people and a clear plan of action with contextually required rules, morals and values drawn up into an agreement,

before you squat. Everyone should sign a copy of this agreement.
• You need to make the owners want you to be there. How will you being there benefit them? This should be well thought through, and you should try and get in touch with this person/these persons once you are in the building and strongly communicate your intent and why it is a good thing.

We were talking for a good couple of hours and he made lots of other points too, but these three points stood out to me so strongly. It was inspiring to have a conversation such as this with someone who has been there and done it and worked out how to iron the kinks. Experience. The conversation unfortunately helped reinforce the perceptions that I had about the reasons things weren't working out as most of us wanted:

"Sounds to me like you need a new place and you need to start again from scratch" He expressed.

"hhhmmmm, perhaps your right. Any suggestions" I half joked.

"Well, funny you should ask, there is one place, I believe it to be one of the oldest buildings in Amsterdam. I wanted to get into it years ago but it never happened. I did some research on it back the and its owned by an old man, there is nothing he can do with it, its location is too tentative, its rotting away. If we were to get in there and start doing the work that the owner can't do then we could be onto something."

I was intrigued, of course I was:

"Can I see it?" I said

"Hell, sure, lets go now. We took the ferry back across to the city and hopped on a tram for a little while. We jumped off in one of the nicest districts in Amsterdam. David took me to the street where the entrance to the building could be fathomed, I looked through the letter box and could see the internal door of which he spoke:

"So, what do you think?" he asked,

"I think I would be interested in looking into this idea further."

"Ok, but you must keep this as low profile as possible."

We agreed to set up a meeting, we agreed on a location, and I was to invite a couple of people along that I trusted and I thought had the mindset for it. I asked David for his email address just in case, he said "You don't need it, I will be there at 8"

That afternoon and evening I was in better spirits. David had refuelled my hope. I thought it would maybe be a good idea to get a couple of people on board from shell, and maybe a couple from Beurspiene. I couldn't wait to mention things to John, Hoda and Gorka, but I didn't want to just mention it to my friends at the 'Great lab', I must say something down at Beursplien too. I took a wander down there to see who was around. The attitude there was beginning to stink in truth, despondency everywhere. I sat down with a group of faces I knew and joined the conversation. I began chatting to one of the lads there that I believed had quite a lot of passion for the cause. He was young, a little younger than me, I didn't always feel as though his perception of people was very accurate and I felt that he could sometimes be very quick to jump to his conclusions, but I trusted him, and felt that inside of a slightly less chaotic, more organised climate, he would thrive. He needed something from his tent and I walked across with him and immediately told him that I had something to discuss with him. A feeling of hypocrisy suddenly shot through me. I thought back to the group of people holding their own meeting instead of joining general assembly, about 'Animal farm'. If I started hand selecting people to come to this meeting with me and David was I not in some way trying to form an elite, just as they had been? Was this what 'Occupy' was about? What was occupy about? What even is occupy again? I was confused. I thought about the differences. I wasn't plotting to oust anyone. This was a new project, in a new place. I thought about whether I was just being too weak in my lack of negative feeling towards Dirk, "The Caveman", after all, if he had taken pipes then maybe he deserved to be ousted? No, there was something too clinical about that. I knew he took some pipes in the first day, he admitted that to me, but I had no reason not to believe him that he had not taken any more, maybe he didn't understand quite the consequences of his actions? Perhaps he had a good heart but just wasn't so bright? Was he just really desperate for money? How much did it really matter in the grand scheme of things? Questions, questions. I couldn't stop from thinking about how things might have been had a living agreement been implemented on the first day they took the shell building. I wondered what the consequences might have been if the group that seemed to be forming an elite had, instead of throwing him out, spoken to Dirk diplomatically, explained, without patronisation, why it causes such a problem if things are stolen and damage is done to a squatted building. To bring it strongly to his awareness. Everybody has their strength, some people have a skill to pick a lock and allow people entrance, and put on a good party. Some people can see more logically and rationally into the world of law and legal matters, both require each other to achieve what I think we might have been trying to achieve. I was still confused. I am a hypocrite, maybe a little, damn, we all are sometimes. Perhaps it was just a justification to myself, but there was a chance to maybe do something that would help our cause, we needed something fresh, David seemed like he knew what he was talking about. If I had to keep the plan quiet for it to have any chance of success then quiet I would be. If I had to approach a handful of people that I trust and not others then I would. Everyone would be given the chance to be involved in the new project if it grew any wings. I didn't feel like David was trying to form an elite:

"What did you want to discuss" the dutchman enquired.

"Well, I met a bloke today who has a lot of experience with squatting in Amsterdam, he took me to a place he wants to take and wants to put a small group together to help take the building. I wondered if you would be interested in coming to a meeting with us in a couple of days?"

"Wow, sounds exciting. Erm….Darn, I have other commitments that night but please keep me in touch with how the meeting goes and what you decide."

I headed back over to shell and found Gorka, John and Hoda in that order. All of them sounded excited by the proposal from David. Gorka would be unable to attend the meeting but wanted filling in on the proceedings, John and Hoda wanted to come to the meeting.

★★★★★★★

I recall not the name of the cafe, but we got a table upstairs. It was private but not claustrophobic, you could overlook the downstairs part of the bar like being up on a balcony. David had been there at 8, John and Hoda and myself were there at 8. We all got a hot drink and began our meet. I guess it was quite formal, I tried to break the ice between David and the others and everyone seemed to be getting on well. David went over afresh all of things he had said to me a few days previous, so as to bring John and Hoda into some form of understanding. Once they had heard what he had to say they seemed even more engaged. In Amsterdam there are still certain squats that have been running for years and years. Once a week a lot of these places hold meetings in particular places where prospective squatters can turn up and talk to experienced squatters, and basically obtain advice. I imagine there would have been a lot more of these types of meetings back when squatting was legal. Anyway, David had been out of the circuit for a few years and decided that we should visit one of these places, there was one on Monday night and we would meet there at 8 again.

On monday morning I woke up and I felt pretty awful. I was finally coming down with a flu. I took a couple of paracetamol and cycled down to the library to send some emails and the such. I began to feel worse. Eventually I decided I needed to head back home. I needed to go to bed. I found John pottering around as usual in the foyer:

"Hey John"

"Hey Ben, everything ok?

"Well not really, I feel pretty sick and we have this meeting with David tonight. If I don't start feeling any better I'm afraid I might not make it"

"Don't you worry about that, you have a rest up and see how you feel later, if you can't make it tonight then don't worry about it, me and Hoda will meet David and give your apologies for not being there"

"Ah thanks John, I will speak with you later"

I went straight to bed and passed out right away. I set my alarm for 6pm, and woke up with a pounding headache as it went off. I sent John a text to let him know that I was out of action for the night. 'No problem', he typed back. I slept straight through to the next morning. When I awoke I felt quite a bit better, the headache had diminished anyway. I sent John a text to see what had occurred at the meeting. To my dismay I found out that John and Hoda had been slightly delayed for whatever reason, something to do with the bikes I think, they got to the meeting at 8.20 anyway, twenty minutes late, and guess what, there was no sign of David. I couldn't believe it, I thought straight away about the day I met David, and how I had asked him for his email address, and he had told me that I didn't need it. How were we to re-establish contact now? Had he been to the meeting? What had he found out? He mentioned something at the cafe about how he had a hunch that the building had a new owner, but he hoped that it didn't because that could have adverse effects on the plan. He would have been there at 8, almost certainly. Did he wait for 15 minutes and then clear off? Did he now think we were unreliable because we hadn't been there on time? Aaaarrrggghhhh. More and more questions that I couldn't get to the bottom of. If only I'd not been ill I would have been there. Blah blah. Sod it I decided, it wasn't meant to be, thats what I told myself.

****

The first party in the building came and passed. It seemed to work. It was quite a low profile and was quite good to get to know people a bit better. Tins of beer were sold, Didi made a small amount of money from working the bar, and a little money was raised. The second party could not be described the same way. It was an after party, going on from 4am on saturday morning, almost into sunday. I knew it was bad news. The parties continued. I dipped in and out of them to see what was occurring. You could feel the positive, demonstrative energy of most people start to fall and crumble into nigh on pure hedonism, part time recreation was becoming full time recreation. Less and less time was being spent thinking about any kind of community matter. People were giving up, handing themselves over to fun, fun? But what kind of fun, a tainted fun I thought, a mask. I pondered about society as a whole. Of course, GET-FUCKED-UP-ISM, that'll fix it eh, well, how can it, it moves us further away, from ourselves, from everyone.

'MURKIER PUDDLES'

Less concentration, bastards packaging more vomit. Fuck. I knew in that moment that all balance was gone. I also knew how my concerns would be perceived.

"Way too serious boy, have a drink, take a sniff, pull more drags"

NO! Fuck, its over, don't they see, don't get me wrong, I love a drag, have a sip, but how much better it tastes after the work is done. The classroom set. The exhibition underway. The seed planted and leaves sprouting. And what did WE have to show, diddly-fucking-squat, that's what: no food, no resources, and now most peoples' minds were out of the equation too.

As I was saying before, it must have been a dream for the police, just waiting, and there we were (collectively) out of it, probably unaware they were even in wait. One tell tale sign that some kind of planned clear out could be imminent was that our basement got closed off. Someone had allowed a group of men in one day who said they needed to seal it off because other peoples things were down there. I knew this wasn't true because most of the stuff had been handed back already. They just didn't want us bunkering ourselves in was all, all they needed to do was pick the right moment. The bleeps of low faith were not intermittent any more, they rung out in one wretched pitch:

'Bbbeeeeeeeeeeeeeeeeeeeepppppp!'

Those that held on too tight could now only torture themselves. Hoda, bless his soul, was one such man, he became drained in a similar way to John had a week or two previously. And of course the 'FUN' of the parties attracted all kinds of characters, mostly benevolent as they were, most just came for some action, no desire to help the cause, just 'party' is all.

It was time to get away for a bit, I hadn't showered or bathed for over a week. I spoke with folk:

"Yes, involved, Occupy"

"Oh I heard about the mayhem"

"Read about it"

Why is it that woe, woe, woe sells a paper. Is that really what most people want, I suppose it may not be a case of want, but that's what we are made to stare into anyway. Scare tactics, so everyone lives in fear, and gets on with their everyday feeding of the system like they are taught to. The "secure" and "safe" option. Am I wrong? That people are taught to live in fear i mean. I fear not.

It felt as if our efforts, all of them, were for nothing. But I know nothing is for nothing, I'd not wasted a second. Could I get up for one more round, if I did it would have to be the last one, for now anyway, illness was on the cards if not. Jonathon was still in cahoots with groups of people, maybe we could still find ways to do some positive work. I spent more time with him and he was kind hearted enough to allow me and Hoda a shower in his house once or twice, and even allowed me to stay there one night when he was out. Bless you friend. I also spent two nights sleeping on the sofa of a girl called Inge, she was not involved with Occupy directly but I met her there. She had been down at the shell building one night with friends for a party, and had found herself in a situation where one of the men at the building (not a resident) started making an unwanted sexual advance towards her. Fortunately there were people around to prevent the situation from escalating and she spent the night safely in the room with a group of residents. I met her the next morning in Hugo's room and made friends. It has to be said that I felt very fortunate to be so welcomed to Amsterdam by so many of its residents, in such a open and understanding way. I truly felt so at home, an Amsterdammer, a tourist breaking out of the tourist hub and seeing the real beauty and collective drive of Amsterdam. It was mentioned to me by numerous locals that Amsterdam is oft referred to as the 'big village', and I really felt why. For such a big place there seems to be such a connectedness somehow, there seems to be a big web, watching each others backs, brothers and sisters caring, just caring.

One night I was cycling over to Jonathon's house in Zeeburg. I had been taking the cycle lanes for a couple of weeks by that point, and as I rode left out of the station a tourist with a huge suitcase bumbled straight into the cycle lane without looking:

"Hey, watch it" I yelled.

I felt enraged and exasperated by the event. 'Maybe I was slightly impatient there', I thought, as I rode on. I had a pang of guilt towards the poor guy. After a few moments of pointing the finger at myself, a big smile started slowly opening up across my face. 'Road rage' I thought, 'bike rage'. 'Damn tourists….haha'. I was at home from home, the feeling felt so natural and unforced, and that was beautiful.

****

After a couple of nights obtaining some perspective within myself, and wandering street markets with my better smelling nether regions, It was decidedly time to open my eyes, breathe deeply and raise myself off the mat one more time. The difference was this time I meant it. One more time that is. I spent the day catching up with people. The parties seemed to still be flowing, if money was being made it was not transparent where it was going. You could sense and see all the segmentation, and I felt an air of deviousness was sneaking in. I was naturally delighted to learn that some wise guy had a key cut for the front door from a key that presumably belonged to a resident. You could now buy your key for 10 euros on the streets of Amsterdam. Roll up, roll up, get on the ride, come and grab yourself a free room down at the old shell building where the fun never stops, PARTY central.

The final insult?

General assemblies were next to impossible to arrange, a rapidly increasing number of people living in, and frequenting the building, had never even heard of general assembly, or any idea resembling it. I went to bed thinking about a train ticket to Manchester.

As I woke I was still not aware that it would be the last time I did so in the building, if I had known, perhaps I would have made a little more of a ceremony of the vague ritual of relighting the heaters, of heating my Chocomel, of breathing in its steam. I wriggled out of my cocoon and started making my way to the cigarette packet on the window ledge. All of sudden came a huge 'BANG', 'BANG', 'BANG' on my door. I turned sharply and headed over to see who was there and what the problem was, but before I could get there the door opened (I must have forgotten to lock it) and in waltzed the 'founding chief'. You remember, the one who was here months before anyone else, 'the despiser of dog shit'. I hadn't seen him for days, weeks maybe. In a rude and impersonal voice he began:

"NO FIRES, NO OPEN FIRES IN ROOMS, YOU CANT HAVE OPEN FIRES IN ROOMS"

The danger of having an open fire in your room had been reinforced to us a few days earlier as people were found to be having big tin drums in their rooms, in which they were inserting wood and burning it, obviously too cold to analyse the danger. I had agreed at the time that using such a heating device was too much of a hazard, and it would not have been something I would have done anyway. It seems Mr Founder had decided to take it upon himself to survey the whole building, bursting in on peoples private dwellings to police the situation. I was in shock:

"I don't have any open fires in my room" I defended.

"What are these then?" he spluttered, pointing at my family of tea light heaters.

"Tea lights inside of brick"

"That is an open fire" he declared.

I let out a frustrated breath and took the lid off the heater nearest to him:

"Look"

"You can't have that" he snarled.

"What do you mean I can't have that, who the hell are you anyway? what right do you think you have barging in to my room, or anyone else's room for that matter, unnanounced, using your tone of intimidation and jumping to conclusions? Are you saying there is a ban on tea lights now?"

"No, you can have tea lights but you can't have those."

"What are you talking about, this is way safer that using a freestanding tea light, the are completely surrounded by brick, I've been using them since I moved into this room weeks ago"

"You can't have them"

He wasn't getting it, I lost my rag:

"Get the fuck out of my room, I don't know how you think you have the right, get out, NOW!"

I ushered him towards the door and he slinked back into the corridor, carrying on telling me that I couldn't have them. The dispute continued for a couple of minutes before Hugo came looking round the corner to see what was going on, he had heard the fracas from his room:

"You ok Ben?" he asked, looking concerned for me.

I explained how 'Mr Founder' had just stormed into my room and started preaching to the converted about open fires in rooms.

"Those heaters are not open fire, they are totally safe" said Hugo, reassuring the founder.

"It is open fire"

He wasn't going to get it, and he'd taken it way too far to admit his mistake. Hugo became frustrated like I was. We stood, and the argument extended for another few minutes before the founder finally waddled off muttering under his breath. I heard all about the situation again later from the rumour mill. "Hugo was intimidating and being violent towards other demonstrators again today, say......violent, danger, oust......! Rumours, rumours, what a service you lend to the manipulate.

I could feel my body, my mind, my soul in anguish. I was 90% sure it was time to go. I had barely enough coin left to even get back to England, it was nearly christmas, I missed a lady. I had no power over things as they stood, to the point where even the personal peace I found in the solitude of my room was being disturbed. I tell you, it was time, I made an instant plan, I'd leave tomorrow, stay in a hostel tonight, come back and grab my stuff in the morning, leave. It pained me so, I didn't want to give up, I can come back in the new year I thought, maybe people will see light, maybe........maybe...........! The dreams had to stay alive. Hope. The dreams must always stay alive, even if they have to be transformed a little, or put in a different place. Just then there was another knock at the door, this time I got to open it myself. In burst Hoda, stick in hand, terror in eyes, slightly out of breath:

"Whats the deal man?" I uttered, worried.

"Four arab guys with swords came into the building this morning with a key they bought off someone. They occupied a room on the top floor. Me and one of the guys went up there and told them that they couldn't just move in like that, they needed to go through general assembly if they wanted to be part of proceedings here. They didn't like that. They pulled swords on us as we ushered them out, and said they would be back to kill me" he cried.

"Oh my god. Sit down brother"

I made him some tea and reassured him that everything was ok. He sat down shaking with his stick still firmly wedged between his fingers. It was only then that it totally dawned on me that the body of 'Our Occupy' was completely dead, all that was left to happen here now was for the leeches and the insects to come in and suck away all the blood from the carcass, and the pigs to devour the rest. I felt so bad for Hoda, he really was doing everything in his power to try and tip the water out of the sinking ship, unfortunately he only had a tea spoon with which to scoop. He had only been here for a number of days and still had a little more fight left in him than some of us. The core of people who had been there from the start, or just after, had depleted perhaps more than I realised. When new people arrived you just got on with it like you did when the old people had been there. It had been a transient environment even from the start, but now it had become a dangerous environment beyond doubt.

****

I rested my head in a shared dorm in the 'stay okay' hostel. The name says it all. It was not a bad place, nor was it great. There was a very chilled woman working on the desk there, we had a decent and understanding chat about squatting. She had been part of the movements in the 90's. I took a well needed shower and put my head down. A couple of people fluttered in and out of the room, grabbing things, using the bathroom, making their beds. I just laid with my head sidewards on the pillow and stared at the wall. I couldn't talk to anyone else, I felt foreign to the joy of that…..my ticket was booked.

I left the stay okay hostel in Zeeburg the next morning, fairly early. Again, I stuffed my pockets with some of the abundant food from breakfast, to distribute at the shell building. As I got off the bus I saw the steps on which I had sat on that day, weeks ago, with all my bags, on my way to the shell building for the first time. I sat down in what seemed to be the exact same spot, lit a cigarette, and reflected. People watching didn't seem to have quite the same beautiful flow to it that day. I walked into the building, climbed the stairs for a last time, wandered around my room for a minute, then picked up my pre packed suitcases. I had a giant wall cloth with a beautiful intricate pattern on it that I had got from the market one day. I should have packed it I suppose, but I didn't. I wanted the room to carry on feeling as homely as It could I suppose. I wanted to come back to it. I hoped I would get the chance. I took out all my bedding and gave it to some of those in need of it, and entrusted the keys for my room and Alex's room to my french friend Louis, telling him to make use of them where possible. I said a couple of sad goodbyes and Louis insisted he walk me to the station to help with my suitcases. We had a coffee and chatted to pass a little time. Prior to me boarding the train we shared a compassionate hug. I dumped my suitcases in the train corridor and sat down with them on the floor, looking out of the train doors at louis who stood waiting for the train to depart. As the doors eased closed so did another chapter. The train took to motion and Louis waved me off. I wished him the best of luck with my intention of thought.

****

Through the puddles of disappointment up darted some large bubble of humanity, they burst out of the stale liquids and sprayed through the air, splashing and reminding us all that it was still alive. Still breathing. Its roots were still clinging on somewhere down deep in the murky depths of the untended puddle. Even if our 'Occupy' was on the rocks, hell, even if it was down on the mat, KO'd, it wasn't the end, it was barely even the beginning. What is 'OCCUPY' anyway? A word. A mish mash of ideas, a plethora of feelings. Its a word we have used since it was born out of the Arab Springs, a word that we have used as a means to make tangible and comprehendible, the beginning of a global rise to put an end to unjust: restriction, greed and deprivation (to name but a few of the issues preventing us from obtaining true freedom together), and whether we succeed in this now or another, the changes that the Occupy movement has tried, somewhat insufficiently, to manifest, will indeed some day reach their manifestation. The virtuous principles relating to occupy are woven deep into the tapestry, a tapestry that we are perhaps only jut beginning to be able to vaguely humanely comprehend right now, but whose beautiful intricate patterns, are hung, with care, all over the interior walls of the divine grand vessel of unsinkable 'LOVE'.

Love it floats,
Love it swims,
Love it flies,
Love is all.

And it started again:

Creeping out of Amsterdam, it begins,
as it has begun so many times before.
I said goodbye to fondant faces in the shell,
with slow wags of a tongue temporarily bruised.
I feel a tainting of a place I hold dear,
a tainting of people and areas acting up, from suppression.
To refresh is to clean without to much conscious thought.

As I watched the flat beautiful lands of Holland pass me by and leave me behind, more words and verses filtered in and out gently:

'Walk, carry, loathe, but then love'

Violent matters I step through and back out,
there are the petulant jabs of the performing monkeys I have yakked of somewhere previously,
but they only ever put their fingers in the blades of our divine spin,
and once they are forced to retract, in blood, in cut, in pain,
the motion of our ethereal vessel will spin once more,
faster and faster until it is part of the furniture.

****

The email arrived, I should have known, how could it not have. It was John:
Hi Ben,

Are you still in England? They sent the MA into the shell building Friday. The copper thieves went crazy and gutted everything. I moved out right before new years. Now living in a Caravan with nice people on about five acres, its nice and warm. Hope all is well with you, and I have never seen David.

Groetjes
John

I found out a week or two later that things were way way darker than this. I understand from a reliable source that when the MA did clear out the shell building, they found someone dead in the party room, needles were scattered, our palace was a crack den. My occupy. Their occupy. OUR OCCUPY. All were over. I don't know exactly how it felt, on the one hand I was completely devastated, I thought I was to return to shell, I wanted to return, there was so much to put right, so much to achieve, so many good people to see again. It hit me all of a sudden that I may never see some of those folk ever again, and that hurt badly. I had shared so much with some of those people. I was sad, but fuck I was angry too, if only those lousy bastards had not fucked it for the rest of us, we could still be there, but no, there was no use to those feelings of anger, it changed nothing, only gave power to things I wished not to give power to, and besides, I couldn't see objectively enough the reasons for the afflictions. Were they all necessary steps? Had we not had clear enough intentions? Probably we hadn't. Was there a distinct lack of understanding? Certainly to a degree. Bad communication? For sure. Were the ones who rubbed our scales in the wrong direction desperate? Some of the homeless were for sure. If that's why they acted the way they did, then how can I feel anger towards that, would I not have acted the same in similar shoes, oh I of slim financial comforts. Understanding!

****

If I am honest, it's nigh on impossible to understand objectively, the complications that caused 'OCCUPY' to breakdown, but I do know that for some reason it broke down, or at least lost momentum, at a similar time, all over the world. One of the main factors, for me, was the fact that we were trying to operate outside of the system that we are still within. This meant that many of us recognised an urge to have no leaders, no dictatorships, no dogmatism. We needed principles, not rules. Had those principles not quite had time to develop and take hold? I don't know. Maybe the capitalist and consumer systems were a little too inscribed into our collective consciousness just yet for us to successfully operate, as a unit, in such a manner. We are, after all, to some degree, products of our environments. Some people are bent on power, that bad strain of power, or moreover the desire of power for personal gain. Immoral power. It's a disease, one of a number of 21st century diseases that we are working on the cure for, and getting there, but not quite. The important thing is that we recognised overwhelmingly, and we recognise increasingly still, that something was, and is, wrong, and more and more people are realising this throughout the world. This is still causing certain negative ramifications and manifestations, but it is my belief that in a larger picture we are moving in the right direction, towards our freedom, towards the freedom of our children, the freedom of our children's children. POSTERITY. In any case, in the direction of lives absent of suppression, of oppression, of depravity. Maybe, in a spiritual and altruistic sense, the idea of trying to outwardly change things invalidated Occupy, to at least some degree, from the outset. Perhaps when we merely concentrate purely on creating the change in ourselves, the rest of the world automatically changes with us. Things are not always as logical as we might think they need to be. This is something that I feel more and more, just as a lot of people are starting to. Maybe it has something to do with a new age, but it feels like something magical is beginning to open, some kind of new opportunity that we have never had access to before, or for a very long time. Maybe occupy played its part in the unfolding on this potential for the masses. I speculate.

During my time with Occupy, as you have probably already figured, it was clear that for whatever reasons, people were still trying to control things, maybe we all were in our own way, and it almost certainly wasn't always free from the derivation of personal pleasure, as opposed to being for the benefit of the community as a collective whole. This was the way it looked anyway. Also notable were a lot of times when people let their own personal emotions lead them to actions that were not beneficial to the community. I feel as though these instances increased as frustration increased. I don't think some of these perpetrators could essentially be labeled power freaks, I think it was more a case of 'seeing red' in certain moments, but their actions were still detrimental to the cause. Such instances again demonstrated our infancy, and lack of ability to work successfully for a cause that perhaps needed to be, in my eyes, at all times, bigger than any of our own personal emotions, mightier than any of our separate egos. Personal disagreements, again in my view, should have been dealt with and resolved by those involved, in a way that was not detrimental and abrasive to what we were trying to achieve.

Maybe confusion also played its part a fair bit, certainly for those who are used to following rules, there was certainly a level of procrastination that could have been enabled due to an absence of order. Maybe self discipline was partly responsible for this, certainly in terms of drug use, but the freezing cold weather (November/December), in conjunction with no heating, in a huge stone building, with next to no resources, all leading to an overall lack of comfort, can all link back into this. In my opinion, as human beings, if we do not have the basic fundamental requirements to live a comfortable life, it is extremely difficult for most of us to move out of survival mode and begin applying ourselves to bigger visions. Maybe this was one of, if not the most important factor that led to the downfall of Occupy, not just in Amsterdam, but all over the world. People in cold tents night after night, with a distinct lack of resources. This will inevitably lead to illness (the cough camp site) and desperation. Perhaps this kind of situation, in terms of similar circumstance, can be applied to the bigger picture of world society (if I can speak of such a thing) as a whole, way beyond Occupy. It seems, to me, pretty obvious and completely viable that most problems of crime, violence and other conflict that we encounter in our world are due to, or at least were born out of, a lack of resources and comfort, which leads to desperation. As has been quoted many times before me "If a man is treated like an animal he will behave like one".

Much of my scribings throughout this book have probably been my own attempts to piece together the reasons why things fell apart, based on observances I made and contemplations I drew from my own personal experience of Occupy. Perhaps Occupy had run its course? Maybe we had drawn what we could from it for now? After all, people all over the world were involved, and we congregated and concentrated, we amplified, we talked, we shared, we achieved (even if it wasn't exactly what we wanted to achieve).

'The underrated mild success'

We grew ourselves, we grew each other, and now we have dispersed again. But we still talk, we still spread, we continue to grow, and whether we are aware of it on not, we have expanded, and continue to expand our own consciousnesses and the collective consciousness, the ripples and waves that we blew across the lake of consciousness are still being felt, lapping gently, and crashing a little more intently where needed. Maybe, we have affected and continue to affect things like the collective consciousness and world soul, just as, I believe, these things affect and connect us. Even if this change was small, it is a step nevertheless.

'The underrated mild success'

The reasons Occupy eventually broke down are perhaps as unclear as the true reasons it started in the first place. It is my view that that there were higher reasons, perhaps beyond our understandings, for both its rise and its fall. Perhaps the world soul (Anima Mundi) was pulling its strings from without, and perhaps even within. Whichever way you look at it, it goes to show just how strong human endeavour can be, how widespread it can become, and how much of a difference it could potentially make, just as it has throughout history, no matter where the strings are ultimately being pulled from.

****

Sitting down with a steamy cup of tea, born from an electrically powered kettle, warm drafts of air came unfolding throughout the house. I sat in my ghastly looking comfort wear with an unshaved face. Nuggets of laughter and love were in my vicinity, and it couldn't help but provide me with some relief, some comfort, some peace, some love. An overwhelming feeling lapped from a thought bobbing inside and all around the outskirts of my head, stroking gently my temples.

In this world full of affliction, of judgement, of diverse ideas, differing utopias, differently textured rights, variously perceived wrongs, it is easy to give up hope of scrambling your shaking body around the upper curved fixture of the ladder, and planting two firm feet onto the safety of the roof. Its easy to forget that feeling of freedom, those harmonious moments when your own subjective personal problems can be viewed like tiny slowly fading candescent leftover dots, mere residue of a largely evaporated nightmare. You stand aloft, wearing the biggest grin of childhood past, knowing and not just wishing that anything is possible, all is attainable. Beaming back out from within (for all to tune into) the pure, sweet, non aspartame, energy of liberation that you have finally received once more into your radio antenna body.

Just what if, instead of tying ourselves down with past afflictions, with concerns of 'too many people', with absurd rationalisations for inhumane greed, what if... instead, we actually got round to making each other the comfiest damn beds we could configure? Collected one another piles of firewood? Gave everyone, yes EVERYONE, on this whole, relatively, dot like planet, the fundamental comfort, and lack of desperation required, to act as a rational human being? Shifting straight past synthesised and outright backward legislation. Without the consuming focus placed on a persons brain capacity, without discrimination against the depth of their skin pigment, their gender, their sexuality, their appearance. "Social status" (think about it, what does that even mean, I mean really), despite blah-de-blah-de-shitting-doo-dah.

Well, this 'what if?' led me systematically to that feeling I had, oh that feeling, you know, the one that stroked my temples. It couldn't help but massage me good. I felt (like a warm sock to cold freshly cut toenails) with some kind of unfathomably deep, almost Johann Sebastian Bach-esque resonance, that an awful lot of doubters, of non see-ers, of non believers, would be incredibly surprised, perhaps stunned, by what we would achieve (If every man and woman were granted foundations that is, as a basic human necessity). The chance for everyone to look beyond survival mode and into the fertile pastures of self realisation.

And oh for them to be granted with love, how immense the power. The secret ingredient. The blessed gift. Maybe you have never thought about it, maybe you gave up, maybe you believe it is of no interest to you. Yet it shone, in that moment, onto my sore retinae like a super charged natural healing flashlight, that despite its affliction, in spite of its confusion, regardless of tampering and of synthesis, the human core, mans natural essence, requires LOVE to unlock anything anywhere near its potential. It turns out that whilst the receiving of love is vital, the spreading of love is just as, if not more crucial. Esoteric science is currently linking the hand of mysticism lovingly, as slowly together, they begin to unfold and explain, to our poor limited minds, such phenomena.

'TO DEPRIVE ANOTHER IS TO DEPRIVE ONESELF' - May the movement of this fact to mainstream common belief and conscious understanding, free us ALL.

Small cogs spinning faster then faster, in increasing concentration. Star clusters adjoining star clusters, black holes marrying black (w)holes, linking slowly up to power the cogs a speck larger, the ones an octave higher. The ones we didn't even know (or moreover forgot), were there.

We were the '99%', and one day we will make it to 100.